To Linda —

Here's to livin, ... r!

The 100% Factor:

Living Your Capacity

Jodee Bock

Bock's Office Publishing

Fargo, North Dakota

Published by Bock's Office Publishing
Fargo, North Dakota

Copyright © 2006 Jodee Bock
3rd Edition – 2008

All rights reserved. No part of this book may be reproduced or
transmitted in any form or by any means, electronic or mechanical,
including photocopying, recording or by any information storage and
retrieval system, without written permission from the author, except
for the inclusion of brief quotations in a review.

Bock, Jodee A.
The 100% Factor: Living Your Capacity/Jodee Bock

ISBN 0-9785722-0-3
ISBN 13: 978-0-9785722-0-4

Third Edition

www.100percentfactor.com
www.bocksoffice.com

Interior layout: Jennifer Munson, 2 J's Graphic Design
www.2jsgraphicdesign.com

Printed in U.S.A.

"If I have the belief that I can do it, I will surely acquire the capacity to do it, even if I may not have the capacity at the beginning."

-Mahatma Gandhi

Praise for <u>The 100% Factor</u>

"Understanding the true nature of who we are is the key to achieving lasting happiness. Although the fundamental nature of life is uncomplicated, we as humans are programmed to make things difficult for ourselves. *The 100% Factor* offers ideas for understanding our true nature and uncovering the wonderful gifts within ourselves."

—**Paul Martinelli**, President, LifeSuccess Consulting, LLC

"The hunger to experience Spirit in the workplace is gaining the force of a movement. The old story of leadership will no longer satisfy this hunger. Followers—employees—are coming to work with a new set of expectations. *The 100% Factor* provides a place where today's untapped capacity as well as tomorrow's potential can become the basis for those new conversations."

—**Dr. Lance Secretan**, Author of ONE: *The Art and Practice of Conscious Leadership* and *Inspire! What Great Leaders Do*

"*The 100% Factor* gives us a simple, inspiring method for turning conventional wisdom into effective practice. It doesn't matter if you know this stuff; the question is: are you doing it? Jodee Bock will show you how."

—**Steve Farber**, Author of *The Radical Leap: A Personal Lesson in Extreme Leadership* and *The Radical Edge: Stoke Your Business, Amp Your Life*, and *Change the World*

"Jodee Bock's message is an important one. She reminds us that we get to decide how good our lives will be. That we're here, not to shrink back and wait for a more convenient time, but to put ourselves and our egos on the line and step forward into the next great segment of our lives."

—**Gail Blanke**, President and CEO of Lifedesigns, LLC, Executive Coach, Motivational Speaker, and Author of *Between Trapezes, Flying into a New Life with the Greatest of Ease*

"Please, read this book! Why? Because you will become a better person after reading it, and you will have an even greater impact on the people you come in contact with each day."

—**Dr. Bob Ash**, Motivational Speaker and Owner of Life Lessons™

"*The 100% Factor* is a must-read for every businessperson, coach, teacher and speaker who wants to reach a new level of personal and professional capacity."

—**Maryanna Young**, President, Personal Value Coaching

"*The 100% Factor* challenges us all to think about what our 100 percent is...and how we can best put that to use. With honest, easy to understand 'reality checklists,' this book is a must-read for all people envious of others. Stop living to others' capacity...increase your own! Read *The 100% Factor* today and use it to change your thinking and your life!"

—**Phil Gerbyshak**, Motivational Speaker and Author of *10 Ways to Make It Great!*

"I so appreciate Jodee sharing her personal stories and inviting me into the conversation by asking questions that inspire me to think. This book provides a gentle yet powerful way of presenting new ways of thinking of old constructs."

—**Susan Ekberg**, Inspirational Speaker and Author

"Great books can be detected by their tattered covers and highlighted pages. *The 100% Factor* will be one of those well-worn books that ordinary people return to time and time again for motivation and practical insights on achieving extraordinary results at work and in life."

—**Kim Fletcher**, Life Coach, Speaker, and Author of *Your Exceptional Life Begins Now*

CONTENTS

PREFACE

T*he 100% Factor* is paradoxical – it's not what you might expect. At first glance you could get the impression that it's about competition and winning, but it's more than that. There is more to life than "winning." That might sound strange coming from an All-American basketball player, I know, but I've learned a lot since those days. And I'll tell you from experience that if you finish the book with the same understanding you had when you started it, then you've missed the major point. If you're not living your maximum capacity, you're cheating yourself.

The 100% Factor is about measuring your own progress against your previous performance. Instead of despairing about how far you have to go, this book will give you a chance to see how far you've come.

You will have an opportunity to examine some of the lessons you've learned over the course of your life, whether at work or outside of work, and ask yourself an important question: "How's that working for me now?"

I can honestly say that in the 18 months since this book was first published, I have grown exponentially in my understanding and application of lessons and situations that have been presented to me in the form of "coincidences" or "chance encounters" or even "mistakes." As I've increased my awareness through study, understanding and time, I've been able to witness and experience many more examples of the effects of new thoughts and ideas on my own capacity.

When I think back on my corporate career, I identify myself as a square peg in a round hole – trying desperately to fit into the mold for which I was hired, and feeling that the only way to do that was to shave off those square corners that made me who I was. It became more difficult to sacrifice those parts of me, even for the pension and benefits, than to be true to who I am. I was taking a paycheck but knowing I was only contributing a portion of myself to the company, despite a connection to the cause. I knew there was more for me to do but didn't yet have the skills or the self-awareness to be able to communicate that to my bosses.

With the benefit of hindsight now, I'm able to see that if I could have created a support system for my seemingly outrageous thoughts and belief system, I may have been able to communicate my ideas in a way that wasn't as threatening as it appeared at the time. Had I known that there were others in the world who shared some of my frustrations about feeling stuffed into the box that was mine on the organizational chart, I may have been able to formulate my thoughts into meaningful dialogue.

It was not my lifelong dream to leave Corporate America to start my own business. But it's my hope that my experiences as an accidental entrepreneur will provide ideas not only for other entrepreneurs, but also for those who choose to stay and make a difference within organizations, whether that is as the entry-level employee or the CEO.

One thing I didn't understand during my corporate career was that 100% is not the same for every person. My 100% may be 50% of what you choose to bring to the situation – or it may be 150% of what you choose to bring. But if we are all committed to bringing our own individual 100% to our work each day – or even to individual projects during the day - and know and trust that our employers, employees, and/or co-workers are doing the same thing, we will have an excellent opportunity to create a higher level of satisfaction at work.

Of course, the opportunity to receive a maximum level of satisfaction from your work will require you to become 100% responsible for contributing your 100%.

In his book *The Four Agreements*, don Miguel Ruiz says one of those agreements is "always do your best." He says that your best will change from time to time depending upon circumstances like your health. But if you can say with all honesty that in every situation each day you did your best, you have nothing to regret.

The feeling you'll have when you connect with something that feels right to you will be like coming home. You'll become more aware of those things you really do know to be true, regardless of what others tell you or what you think you should be or do.

Getting beyond the victim mentality is tough. But as tough as it is to be 100% responsible, and in spite of the inner struggles I still occasionally face, I'd choose being responsible for my own results a million times over feeling like my future is in someone else's hands. If I continue to leave situations when they get tough without resolving my disparities, I'll be living that old adage "wherever you go, there you are." I realize, with surprising clarity, that that has been my pattern: to leave when things get tough instead of making a difference where I am.

So my pledge is to offer suggestions that will support people who want to make a difference wherever they choose to be, whether that is within an organization or on their own. There is definite power in numbers. Make a pact with yourself to get together with others who share your quest and start a dialogue.

This book provides examples of conventional wisdom that you've undoubtedly heard over the years of your life. Conventional wisdom is great, but it's just that: conventional. When you start examining ideas and concepts in totally new ways, you might have an opportunity to move into a more unconventional way of thinking – and a way that may connect for you more effectively.

On the other hand, be careful not to discount advice or adages just because they may not be current. Some of the statements might still fit, some might not. It's up to you to decide. Ancient wisdom is still around because it's effective. Human beings in our day and age share the same biological makeup as our ancestors and forefathers and foremothers. It would serve us very well to study some of the foundational wisdom they've shared with us over the decades, centuries and even millennia.

Recognizing areas where we'd like things to be different is the first step, but it's not enough to just think about taking those steps. We've got to do something with what we know.

You may already know this stuff, but I challenge you to think of the conventional wisdom without the filters you've gotten used to over the years. And don't forget about being open to some new ideas as well. As Doris Lessing says:

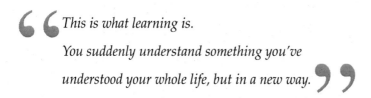

This is what learning is.
You suddenly understand something you've
understood your whole life, but in a new way.

Here's to learning—and taking your knowledge from idea to action!

The 100% Factor

INTRODUCTION

I'll bet there was a time in your life when someone said you had a lot of potential. On the surface, that could sound like a compliment, but when you really start to think about it, what does that say about your current level of performance? If you have a lot of potential, does it mean that maybe someday you'll live up to it, but it's not happening now?

Maybe as a young person that's a great thing to recognize. After all, young people haven't had time to develop too much personal experience.

But for those of us who have been around for a while, what are we waiting for? If we're still seeing ourselves in the eyes of potential, when might we choose to start living it?

That's the distinction between potential and capacity. If I've got a 12-ounce cup of coffee, that cup's capacity is 12 ounces. That's the maximum amount it can hold. If the cup is 100% full, it's (figuratively) living its capacity.

How many of us can say that we are living our capacity? Potential is somewhere off in the future. But is the future really sure? All we really have is today. So if we're living in someday, we're living in potential.

I've spent a good portion of my life in love with the potential - in personal relationships, business relationships, career opportunities - but have only recently begun to see that that isn't always the reality. The reality is right here, right now, today: the capacity.

I made the decision in 2003 to leave Corporate America and join a partner in an entrepreneurial venture providing leadership training and development. There really isn't a story to how I made the leap, but I guess that is the story. I had no idea what it meant to become a business owner, but I just knew that I couldn't keep doing things the way I had been doing them in my career.

Armed with very little savings (what, me plan?) and a contract that would pay the mortgage for four months, I ventured out to a land without time clocks, without weekly meetings, without required reports - and without a regular paycheck and all the other benefits I had taken for granted for so many years as I struggled to reach that ever-elusive potential.

In 2005 I made the decision to form my own independent company called Bock's Office Transformational Consulting, which continues to surprise and amaze me. Through several experiences and some not-so-easy life lessons, I've come to the point where I choose to live my life each and every day at 100% capacity, whether that's a 12-ounce cup or a gallon jug. I think as we grow and learn and evolve in our thinking and our ways of being, we move from the 12-ounce cup to the 20-ounce cup to the 32-ounce cup and eventually, wherever our capacity takes us. But it doesn't have to be an immediate jump from one to the other. That's where we might get hung up. Comparing the size of our cup to another's can have us focusing backward instead of on the reality of the present.

Maybe the goal should be for each of us to examine our container (whether it's 4 ounces, or 12 ounces or 10 gallons) and determine whether we're living at full capacity. What is your 100%? If we can all figure out first what that 100% is and feels like, and then figure out how to give that - or just to be aware how much of the percentage we're comfortable giving - we can find that place where we know we're doing our best. If we can alter the size of the container as we become more proficient at certain tasks, we don't have to worry about living half a life or wasting our efforts by overflowing the container.

The 100% Factor will inspire people at any stage of their lives to consider the opportunities they can create when they re-examine their capacity, and become mindful about how much of that capacity they choose to bring – to work, to relationships, to families.

Some may choose to leave the best part of themselves in the car in the parking lot, just waiting for the end of the day when they can become 100% again. Some may choose to start with a smaller cup, fill that, and then move on, always living at current capacity. The choice is always there.

Each section of the book offers ideas and stories in areas you may want to consider as you determine your capacity. They do not need to be read sequentially, so pick the section that applies to an area you're interested in learning more about for yourself and experiment.

At the end of each section is a reality checklist so you can determine what you really want in your life as it relates to that particular section. As Oprah's fitness guru Bob Greene says, "If we don't know what we want, we become like a floating balloon. Our direction in life is at the mercy of external forces." It's a little like getting in your car and just driving without a destination. You'll end up wasting time and gas without any idea where you are or how you got there.

Once you've determined what you want, ask yourself what you're doing to get that. Then ask yourself how what you're doing is working. If it's not working, ask yourself – or some trusted advisors – what you could do differently. That question opens up space for solutions instead of focusing on the problems or on what's not working.

As you play around with those questions, you can alter the first one from "what do I want?" to "what do I intend?" and then on to "to what am I committed?" Each of those questions gives a different perspective to the task at hand and can provide new ways of getting to the outcomes you desire.

Whatever your role within an organization, *The 100% Factor* will give you fresh perspectives on ordinary concepts and ideas to help create a new attitude about the world of work and the world outside of work. By supporting employees in bringing 100% of themselves to work, employers can expect at least 100% return on their investment. By examining and then producing their own 100% with each task or project, employees will step into their personal responsibility. This book guarantees no answers, but provides stories, analogies, new perspectives – and lots of questions - that will inspire the reader to action in making a difference both inside and outside the workplace.

WARNING:

You already know the stuff in this book. You just forgot.

Remembering may compel you to do something differently.

Once you recognize the distinctions this book will point out,

you can't go back to the same way of being—

in your work or in your life!

The CAPTIVE PAST

"Those who don't learn from the past are destined to repeat it."

~ Your History Teacher

Mama said there'd be days like this. But how often do we let what Mama said – years and years ago – hold us back today?

Dr. Phil calls these defining moments – the episodes in our past that make us who we are today. They served us very well - at the time. Consider the age you were and the life stage you were in when you made those decisions that have now formed your current reality.

I learned to read at age 3. My mother was tutoring a 6-year-old boy, in our home, who had been involved in an accident and couldn't go to school for a period of time. While learning to read was part of what he had to do as a first-grade student, from my pesty 3-year-old perspective, it was just fun.

So I learned to read and my entire world opened up. I read everything I could get my hands on. I'm certain I was even more of a challenge to my parents with this new skill than I had been as a precocious kid who couldn't read.

By the time I got to first grade, all of what we were learning was old hat to me. In fact, I remember the very day the teacher pulled out the reading books thinking to myself "today *they* get to learn to read."

By this time my mother had returned to her fourth-grade teaching position, and one day I overheard my first-grade teacher talking to my mom about how she thought I should skip first grade and go directly to second grade. I remember my mom said no. I'm sure there was much more to that conversation, but that's all I remember, and in my 6-year-old head, that meant I wasn't good enough. From then on I can remember trying to do everything I could to be good enough. No, not just good enough, but better than everyone else.

This new-found competitive spirit served me very well – for a while. I excelled in school, and eventually in sports - in the activities that rewarded external behaviors. But I didn't have many friends because I was the kid other mothers wanted their kids to be like. Who wants to be friends with someone your parents like? I actually had one friend whose mother would drop her off at my house to play and then that friend would leave my house and go hang out with her other friends, sneaking back to my house in time for her mom to pick her up.

I thought everyone was driven to making everything they did better, so I never understood why my classmates weren't spending as much time as I was on school projects and homework and were spending their time playing.

Things got a bit out of hand when I threw a book at one of my friends in 7th grade and hit him in the head because he got a better grade on a paper than I did. But even that realization didn't change my nature. It carried over to my college experience and even into my career. I was always looking to make things better and I was driven to enter contests so I could win awards and prove to everyone that I was good at what I did. I read books and magazine and articles so I could quote other people's ideas. This would allow me to seem well-read and intelligent, but if you didn't like what I had to say, I could hide behind someone else's thoughts. If you rejected me, it was only because you didn't really know me – you knew who you thought I was because it was who I let you know.

Only when I realized that this ultra-competitive attitude was created by 6-year-old me was I able to see from a new perspective how perhaps the adult me might make new choices about living free from those characteristics that had served me well at very different times in my life.

The past really does have a lot to do with who we are today, but it doesn't have to hold us to something we chose in very different times or circumstances. If we don't begin to recognize our own opportunities to alter the things that frustrate us the most in our lives, we'll be destined to see our future through the eyes of our past.

What is holding you back? What served you well at the time, but is no longer working for you?

If we don't learn from the lessons the past has taught us, we will be given many more opportunities to learn those lessons. It really is amazing how readily those pesky life lessons can appear - and how prevalent they are when we have something to learn! Did you ever wonder why the exact same situation can totally tick one person off while another person in the same environment doesn't even notice? That's a fancy gift-wrapped lesson with the personalized card on it. The situations which bug us the most are the ones with the most important, and often the most pressing, lessons for us to learn.

Some situations might appear in more than one package. They might not look the same on the outside (one's got a gold bow and one's got a red bow, for example), but the lesson inside is remarkably similar. Until we figure out why these gifts are still being presented to us, we'll be destined to keep unwrapping the packages, hoping to find new gifts inside, but finding the exact same thing in the box.

It's not enough for us to say to ourselves "I've already got one of these"... we've got to really accept the gift for what it is: a lesson for our entire lives. When we understand that we have a choice to really accept the gift as a gift, not a reprimand, an "I told you so" or a form of punishment, we can get beyond this gift and beyond the situation that presented it to us, and on to other opportunities to learn and apply.

The challenge with learning something new is that once you hear it, you need to actually do something with it. The true test will be whether you're presented with this gift yet again. Isn't it time you got a brand new one? Or better yet – don't wait for someone else to give it to you ... go out and get it for yourself!

The past is passed. You've experienced something. You've learned something. How's it working for you in the present? Be honest with yourself and see whether you're holding yourself hostage to your past. What worked for you before might not work for you anymore. Are you staying in the familiar at the expense of a brand new (and even better) experience?

Try something new today. Listen to a new radio station when you get in your car. Or better yet, turn the radio off and notice what you notice when you're driving. Take a deep breath while you're gripping the steering wheel. Notice how shallowly you usually breathe. Look around at the landmarks and countryside you usually take for granted. Or get out of the car altogether and go for a walk. I'll bet you'll see something for the first time that's been there all along.

How's that for a new perspective?

REALITY CHECKLIST

(complete and repeat as needed)

What keeps happening in my life that keeps me stuck? Where might my past be holding me back from living at full capacity? _____

_____

_____

_____

What am I doing to get unstuck? _____

_____

_____

_____

_____

How is it working? _____

_____

_____

_____

_____

What might I do differently? _____

_____

_____

_____

_____

The FEAR FACTOR

"We have nothing to fear but fear itself."

~ Franklin D. Roosevelt

I f we're brutally honest with ourselves, we might be surprised to discover how much of our lives is run by fear. Fear in our lives runs the gamut from phobia to anxiety and depression to a debilitating mental illness that prevents some of us from living a normal life. Sometimes we are frightened by concepts or conditions or feelings we can't even articulate. Sometimes we are unnerved by situations and circumstances we don't even recognize. We may not even realize that our behaviors are stemming from fear until we stop and think about it.

At its most basic level, fear is the perception of external threat to one's physical safety or well being. This can be an authentic threat (being in the direct line of a tornado) or an inauthentic threat (not attending an outdoor concert because, even though it's a sunny day with no rain in the forecast, it still could rain). Both authentic and inauthentic threats produce the same biological reaction in our bodies.

When we allow ourselves to operate in fear mode, we revert to our reptilian brain – that "fight or flight" mode. From the reptilian brain we get the character traits of cold-blooded behavior, the desire for top-down hierarchy, and an obsession with ritual.

Examples of reptilian brain behaviors:

- Road rage
- Protecting our territory (or our relationships)
- Taking orders without thinking
- Reacting to circumstances in a predictable manner

The reptilian brain never learns from experience. Operating in reptilian mode destines you to repeat the same behavior over and over. Fear keeps us in reptilian mode and fear is a powerful beast. It holds us in its grip and squeezes the rationality right out of us, in many cases.

We're afraid of so many things that just don't make any logical sense in our adult lives. We're afraid of speaking up in a meeting at work, even though we know others could benefit from our comments or questions. We're afraid of not being perfect. We're afraid that others will laugh at us. We're afraid we will trip on the way to accepting an award. We're afraid we'll be swallowed up by an earthquake (even though we live in a part of the world that has never seen an earthquake).

If we're living our lives in fear of things that most likely will never happen, we're really living only a portion of our lives. And it's probably not even the most effective portion. Like my high school basketball coach used to say, instead of playing to win, we're playing not to lose.

There is a time and a place for fear in our lives. Nature has created fear to help the young of any species survive. Yet most of the things adults fear are based on experiences they've had in their past – things which served them well as children, but which now hold them to behaviors which no longer are appropriate.

In our adult lives, we are governed by two big fears: fear of failure and fear of embarrassment. If we are afraid of being embarrassed or treated as failures, we won't be living our capacity. We won't take risks. We will act only on what we know, and what we know resides in our past. These fears don't have anything to do with what's happening right now – in the present. They are only imagined threats that aren't even happening, but are keeping us from acting in the most effective way.

When we have a fear of failure, we either take action or don't in order to avoid failure in the future. Remember: what we resist persists. By resisting failure, we keep it always with us.

You have failed in the past – we all have. But we're still here. We survived that failure. Why in heaven's name if we're so afraid of failing again, do we keep carrying it with us? If it's a failed relationship, why do we give so much power to that relationship by dragging it along through our next relationship?

And these relationships can be found everywhere, not just in our personal lives. Think about the relationships we have at work. If we're living in fear at work, where we really do spend a majority of our waking hours, that fear-based behavior will undoubtedly carry over into the rest of our lives.

According to corporate coach Jan Austin (www.potentialatwork. com), some common symptoms of fear at work include:

- "Us versus them" talk

- Silence during meetings, but widespread talk outside of meetings

- Widespread poor morale

- Resignation, wish for retirement or layoff

- Resistance to new ideas

- Overactive rumor mill

- Lack of input or suggestions for improving working conditions

- Lowered productivity, increased mistakes/waste

- Increased absences and tardiness

- Reluctance to admit mistakes

- Tendency to blame the environment or others for a host of issues

- Denial of tensions and conflicts which are at or near the surface

What do we do to get beyond the grip of fear in our overall lives? The first step is to recognize the fear we have in any given situation. Is it authentic? Is it a threat to our physical well being? Or is it a projection of something which might not (probably won't) even happen?

As we begin to target our fears – in the workplace, in our relationships, in our families – we can begin to dismantle the ones that don't serve us anymore.

I remember a television commercial not so long ago where a mom wraps the kid in bubble wrap because she's so afraid he's going to get hurt. The kid goes through his daily routine at school hardly able to wiggle a finger, but mom feels better because she's been able to protect him. Another television commercial I've seen has the dad reading a bedtime story to the little boy and after every phrase the boy asks his dad if the characters in the book have checked the smoke detector – if they've made sure the door is locked – if they've put away all the utensils that could be dangerous. The dad is thankful that the little boy learned about safety at school because he's able to help them prepare their home for the insurance they need. It's one thing to be cautious; it's another thing to be obsessed.

Of course, there are times and places for varying degrees of what could be considered fear. These include worry and concern. But if we consider the distinction even between those two terms we might see that it's not actual fear that we need to be so gripped by.

Worry implies a strong feeling of anxiety, trouble, distress, uneasiness. When we worry, we carry unnecessary stress because more often than not, the matters we worry about never happen.

Concern is often used as a synonym for worry; however when we consider the actual definition, concern simply means "to have to do with, or be related to; to have regard for or interest in someone or something."

To be worried about something often takes up unnecessary negative energy while to be concerned with something doesn't necessarily have the same negative connotation attached to it.

When we really think about it, didn't FDR have it right? But we've got it backwards. The way we've got it going in our lives is that it's the effects of the potential fear that scare us so much, not the fear itself. I have a friend who says she is afraid of being a chicken. It's not anything external that causes her fear – it's her fear of being afraid. If we can identify our fears to that level, we might be able to see that really, there is nothing external that is causing our risk aversion or our lack of being fully present in our own lives.

There certainly is a place for authentic fear in our lives. The adrenaline rush we get in times of real crisis can serve us very well in the face of a burning building or a charging grizzly bear. We've all heard the stories of the 120-pound woman who lifts a car to save her child pinned underneath.

But if we're allowing our reptilian brain to take over when we're at the office or in the midst of a passionate dialogue with a friend or family member, we may not be using the best part of ourselves.

In Neale Donald Walsh's book *Communion With God*, God claims that the presence of fear draws to you that which you fear. "Fear is a strong emotion, and strong emotion – energy in motion – is creative. ...The way to live without fear is to know that every outcome in life is perfect."

Another way to think of fear is by considering it as an acronym: False Evidence Appearing Real. Here's another excerpt from *Communion With God*:

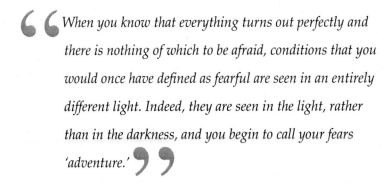

When you know that everything turns out perfectly and there is nothing of which to be afraid, conditions that you would once have defined as fearful are seen in an entirely different light. Indeed, they are seen in the light, rather than in the darkness, and you begin to call your fears 'adventure.'

So think about the areas you are letting fear get in the way of being the most effective you can be. Is it an authentic fear or a fear of something that's occurring only in your mind? Step outside what's comfortable for you. If you're stopped in something you need to say, practice on a trusted friend. Invite her or him to join your "team" as a coach or an advocate for the you you know is inside just trying to come out.

Just noticing whether what you're feeling is indeed fear or whether it's worry or concern will help you determine what to do with what your body is feeling. Authentic fear (caused by a fire in your home or a grizzly bear running at you on a camping trip in the woods) is one thing, but an obsession with alien abductions is another.

Perhaps it really is as Marianne Williamson described in *A Return to Love,* and as Nelson Mandela borrowed for his inaugural address, and as the young basketball player quotes in the movie Coach Carter: our deepest fear may not be what we think it is.

"Our deepest fear is not that we are inadequate. Our deepest fear is that we are powerful beyond measure. It is our light, not our darkness that most frightens us. We ask ourselves, Who am I to be brilliant, gorgeous, talented, fabulous? Actually, who are you not to be? You are a child of God. Your playing small does not serve the world. There is nothing enlightened about shrinking so that other people won't feel insecure around you. We are all meant to shine, as children do. We were born to make manifest the glory of God that is within us. It is not just in some of us; it is in everyone. And as we let our own light shine, we unconsciously give other people permission to do the same. As we are liberated from our own fear, our presence automatically liberates others."

–Marianne Williamson *A Return to Love*

REALITY CHECKLIST
(complete and repeat as needed)

What are my fears, both in my work and in my life? _____

_____

_____

_____

_____

What am I doing to get beyond those fears? _____

_____

_____

_____

_____

How is it working? _____

_____

_____

_____

_____

What might I do differently? _____

_____

_____

_____

_____

The CHALLENGE OF CHANGE

"Change never lasts."

~ You, from experience

What is it about the concept of change that has such a hold on our human lives? Almost everyone has some reaction when faced with change. Some of us are enlivened; some of us are intimidated; and some of us are absolutely petrified of having to do something different. We get so set in our ways that we don't even see that a new way to do something could offer an even better outcome. Or maybe we do see it, but our pride won't let us admit it.

Yet, on the other hand, we are a quick-fix society. We have instant oatmeal, minute rice, fast food, even drive-up insurance. Once we decide we want something, we want it now.

That's how we're really funny about change. If we decide we want something to be different in our own lives, we'll do anything to have that change made overnight. Get rich quick. Lose 10 pounds while we sleep. We'll fall for anything that promises that instant change.

But when someone else imposes change on us against our will or without our knowing, we'll scratch and claw and fight to keep things just as they've always been – even if the new way would really be better for everyone concerned. This seems more often the case in our work settings.

Our bosses, managers, parents, preachers, teachers – really, anyone in authority – often make decisions that involve us without telling us. New work orders, new reporting structures, new software packages, vacation plans, pop quizzes – none of these changes feel particularly positive. Even if we know the decision is the "right" one, we will still resist because we weren't given a chance to voice our opinion. We hate having someone else tell us what we need to do – and what we need to change.

So change has gotten a bad rap. Overall, in our lives, we hate it. I used to believe the only time we would change anything would be to avoid pain. We'd make the switch when the pain of staying the same became greater than the pain of changing. But I think we're starting to choose familiarity over comfort. We'd prefer to sit in uncomfortable familiarity than make a change – even one that might provide better results.

Well, let's cut ourselves some slack. After all, our own gravity wants to keep us the same. Our built-in humanity will much prefer the status quo.

My blogging buddy Alexander Kjerulf says that change really is a paradox, whether it's change inside ourselves or in the world. He says the first paradox is, of course, that these two types of change are intimately intertwined. There is no change out there without change in here. Which is why he says the roadblocks we put in our own way often matter more than the ones outside of ourselves.

What if we just accepted the fact that change – as we currently know it - never sticks?

Change doesn't stick because change is nothing more than more of the same. For example, if I wanted you to give me "change" for a quarter, and I asked you for the easiest way to do that, you might give me two dimes and a nickel. That's change, all right. But let's say I didn't like that combination, and wanted something different. You might give me a dime and three nickels. If that doesn't satisfy me, you might give me five nickels.

We could keep playing this "change" game until you'd finally given me 25 pennies. Change? Sure. But each time all I've really gotten is more and more of the same stuff (and heavier pockets).

If we really want something to be different in our lives, it's got to go beyond mere change. In the above example, what's missing is the key component to what's missing in any situation in which we want something to be different: the element of giving something up. In order for us to make a significant alteration in that change cycle that doesn't work, we have to be willing to give something up. In the 25 cents example, that means I have to be willing to completely give up my 25 cents (in whatever combination I'm left with) and replace that with something completely new (like a pencil or a piece of gum).

That, I propose, is what's been missing in our quest for change:

the concept of giving something up in order to get something new that lasts over time.

So, what will it take? Well, for one thing, we can never change someone else. I know people who spend inordinate amounts of time and energy trying desperately to change others. This could be a spouse, partner, employee, boss, sibling – really, any other person. It's never going to work. But the twist is that as we see an opportunity to shift our own thinking about ourselves and our own perspective, others around us will appear to change.

Situations that used to frustrate or upset you as they relate to other people will stop affecting you once you stop trying to change them. In that way, your attitude will "change" others. The energy and effort you waste in trying to get others to change can be much better applied to the only person you really can affect and that's you (and for me, it's me!).

When you focus your efforts where you can make a difference, it's amazing how different your perspective about everyone and everything else will look. In that way, they do appear to change.

But what happens more often is that the stuff that doesn't work in our lives just goes on and on because nobody's able to be "the enemy." However, it is those "enemies" – those agents of lasting change – who actually provide the greatest vision for the future of an organization in transition. It is these "enemies" who understand the importance of speaking the truth, and remaining committed to that truth. They are the ones who will support the organization in setting the foundation for lasting change because they understand that the current problems they face cannot be solved at the same level of thinking that created them, to paraphrase Einstein.

Seth Godin, in his book *Survival is Not Enough,* talks about how our organizations need to consider evolution, which is permitting change to occur, not fighting it. He says we need to train people (or train ourselves) to make small, effortless changes all the time. This is what Seth calls "zooming." Then we can build a company that zooms and that attracts zoomers. As the company or organization gathers steam, it will enter runaway, by embracing changes that will inevitably come.

He says that zooming is about stretching your limits without threatening your foundation. It's about handling new ideas, new opportunities, and new challenges without triggering the change-avoidance reflex.

Start practicing ways to zoom within your work and home environments by trying new things. When you decide to do something new, you don't have to make a 180-degree shift – even one degree can make a huge difference in the big picture. After all, it is only one degree that makes the difference between water that steams and water that boils. Moving a telescope's viewfinder by centimeters may give a view of a whole new galaxy.

Think about asking the question "Why?" when someone tells you there is a certain way to do things. Then ask it again in response to the answer. And repeat the question until you've gotten to the core, the basic truth, the real reason for avoiding change - or for promoting it. Either way, you'll be certain about your position.

Dr. Wayne Dyer shares a story from his childhood in several of his speeches. He grew up in a series of foster homes, and one day when he was in the third grade, he came home to ask the woman who ran one of the foster care facilities he was living in if she knew what a scurvy elephant was. She said she had never heard of such a thing and asked Wayne where he had heard it. Wayne said that he had overheard his third-grade teacher telling the principal that Wayne was a "scurvy elephant" and he wanted to know what it was.

When Wayne's house mother asked the teacher, the teacher replied that she hadn't called Wayne a "scurvy elephant" – she had said that Wayne was a "disturbing element" in her classroom.

What would we do without the disturbing elements in our world? We would never have anyone willing to question the status quo. We would have even more people who go along to get along. More people who cover up truth within organizations because they're afraid to speak up. More of the same – or, as the next story illustrates, more copyfrogs.

In his book *Inspire! What Great Leaders Do*, Lance Secretan says that according to old urban legend, if you drop a live frog into a pot of boiling water, the frog will jump out. But if you drop the frog into a pot of cold water, put it on the stove and turn up the heat, the frog will cook to death. You may think the frog might wonder why no one else is saying anything about the increasing temperature but be too embarrassed to say anything itself until it's too late. Lance says that when you combine that frog with the copycat, who does things just because everyone else does, you get the copyfrog – "someone who is afraid to speak up for fear of ridicule or feeling alone, or appearing not to be a team player, even though many others may feel the same way, and are also afraid to speak out."

Even though it may be difficult, in order to get new results in our lives, we might have to think about changing our old ways. Have you ever seen those money booths at trade shows and on game shows?

You go into these booths where there are dollar bills blowing around and you have to catch as many as you can in a certain amount of time. If you grab two handfuls, that's the physical limit for you - you can't get any more unless you loosen your grip on what you've got. I've seen people stuff those dollar bills in their shirts, pants, wherever they can as they grab for more before time runs out. But in order to grab for more, they had to let go of what they had.

Think of the dollar bills in this analogy as old ways of thinking. We can't gain any new knowledge or experience without letting go of some of the old.

It may take some courage to question the status quo, but if you don't, you may end up where you are headed. We've all got to be willing to be – and to support – the scurvy elephants in our lives, or else we need to be ready to face a world of copyfrogs.

REALITY CHECKLIST

(complete and repeat as needed)

Overall, how do I feel about change? How do I accept or deal with changes that I can't control? _____

_____

_____

_____

What am I doing to see change through a new lens? _____

_____

_____

_____

_____

How is it working? _____

_____

_____

_____

_____

What might I do differently? _____

_____

_____

_____

The AUTHENTICITY AFFAIR

"To thine own self be true."

~ William Shakespeare

How can we be authentic when we're living as a captive to our past and are burdened by fear?

Authenticity is an easy word to define but can be a difficult concept to grasp and apply to our lives. Dictionary.com defines authenticity as:

1. Conforming to fact and therefore worthy of trust, reliance, or belief.
2. Having a claimed and verifiable origin or authorship; not counterfeit or copied.

How does that apply to our lives? We can believe we are being authentic, but how many of us really know what that is for ourselves?

It reminds me of an interview Oprah did with John F. Kennedy Jr. shortly before he died. She asked him if he remembered much about his father. John said he wasn't sure whether he actually remembered the events themselves or whether it was the memories he'd made from the many photographs he'd seen of those events.

If we spend the early parts of our lives trying to please others and trying to be what others expect us to be, we'll be living inauthentic lives in relation to what we really are. Even as children we are asked what we want to be when we grow up, and are never asked or affirmed for what we already are.

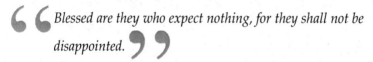 *Blessed are they who expect nothing, for they shall not be disappointed.*

—Carl Sandburg

The first time I heard this quote, I thought it was rather depressing. I remember thinking that if we don't expect anything from the people in our lives, they will never rise to any level of accountability.

But the more I've thought about it, the more I see that this is really a very positive statement. Who am I to set an expectation for someone else according to my standards anyway?

If I go into every encounter with an expectation, I'm sure to be disappointed. After all, as a recovering perfectionist, I see much more clearly now how difficult (if not impossible) it is for anyone (including me) to live up to a level that by its very definition is impossible to achieve.

If we live in what we think we should be instead of what we are, then we are in a constant quest for looking good. Even when it's just us, we don't know how to recognize our true selves. Standing naked in front of the mirror, we can't bring ourselves to see who we really are because we see ourselves through eyes that have been jaded to distort reality through eyes of expectation.

In my understanding of this context, having a clear-cut expectation uncovers a level of attachment to an outcome which should look a certain way.

What if we gave up attachment to how something should be done or how it should look, and instead concentrated on our commitment to having something happen? If we're committed to or taking a stand for something we believe in, and if we can give up how it should look, we can keep our determination without setting ourselves up for disappointment.

Have you ever considered the circumstances surrounding your birth? I was born in a small North Dakota town on January 4 at 4:10 p.m. At that moment in time, I was the only person in the entire universe to have been born in that place. The way the stars and planets were aligned at that very moment in time was not the same for anyone else before or since. It may sound rather obvious, but to me, that means that I have a unique place in the universe that no one else can fill. It's my opportunity to determine how I can live into my destiny as authentically as I possibly can. Each of us is given unique gifts and has a purpose to fulfill whether we realize it or not. If we don't fulfill our own unique purpose, no one else can.

Steve Farber, a former member of the Tom Peters staff, has written a really fun book called *The Radical Leap*. It's a parable about leadership and in the book there is a story about a guy who is trying to reach another guy. He calls, and the answering machine picks up. Here's the message on the machine:

> 'You may think this is an answering machine. It is not. This is a questioning machine. And there are two questions: Who are you? and What do you want? And lest you think those are trivial questions, consider that most people go through their entire lives without ever answering either one.'
> Beeeep.

This is such an important message, and one that few of us ever do stop to consider in our lives. Just taking time to really consider the questions "Who are you?" and "What do you want" will help us to connect with our own unique attributes and as we work on those questions, we can get more comfortable with who we really are.

Henry David Thoreau was a great example of someone who lived an authentic life. He was born in 1817 and lived his entire life true to what he believed, even though it meant that he went to jail rather than pay taxes to a government that supported slavery. He eventually built his own small house on the shores of Walden Pond, outside of Concord, Massachusetts, where he wrote several essays, among them *On the Duty of Civil Disobedience* and *Walden*. One of his most famous quotes comes from the conclusion to *Walden:*

> ❝ Why should we be in such desperate haste to succeed and in such desperate enterprises? If a man does not keep pace with his companions, perhaps it is because he hears a different drummer. Let him step to the music which he hears, however measured or far away. ❞

Being truly authentic is not an easy concept, but one that will allow a huge breakthrough for you in your life. As you stop trying to be something someone else thinks you should be, you start living your life.

It's taken me a few years of concerted effort, but I've determined for myself that my purpose in this lifetime is to promote bigger small talk. In fact, I've created an event where I invite people from all over the world to come to the Summit for Bigger Small Talk here in Fargo, North Dakota.

At this event I'm able to surround myself with others who share in the quest for practicing "riskful" thinking as opposed to merely "wishful" thinking. They all get to be in a safe space to practice conversations that matter, and then take their learning back to their families, their workplaces, their communities, and the world. (For more information about the Bigger Small Talk Summit, visit www.biggersmalltalk.com.)

I recognize that there are certainly areas in my life where I could be better (some call these "weaknesses," but I choose to look at them as "growth opportunities"), but that when I'm freed up to concentrate on my strengths and to identify with who I was born to be, those growth opportunities will take care of themselves.

Of course, this has been a process in my life. I wasn't always so attuned to my own purpose. But when I really began paying attention to what I was starting to understand, I noticed messages appearing everywhere. One of the most striking examples happened to me one day as I was listening to a local talk radio program in my car and was jolted awake by what I heard about myself.

I wasn't in the habit of listening to this particular radio show, even though I did know one of the hosts of the show. But one morning I found myself very intrigued by the conversation the hosts were having with an author named Gail Blanke. They were interviewing her about her book called *Between Trapezes: Flying Into a New Life With The Greatest of Ease*, which addresses life transitions. The book sounded fascinating to me, and I was really listening closely, when the host of the show said right out loud on the air: "This reminds me of Jodee Bock. She's someone who, whenever I'm around her, always makes me feel better about myself."

I was floored. Not only had the radio host mentioned me, she had mentioned me in the context of this author she was interviewing – this author who had not only written a wonderful book, but, according to the interview, had even sat on the couch with Oprah on her show!

Well, you can bet I hightailed it back to my office and immediately called Gail Blanke (you never know what can happen when you pick up the phone!). When I did get through to her, I told her that I was the person they had mentioned during the interview and after talking with Gail for a few minutes, I can remember her saying, "We have a lot of work to do with our coaching businesses." Wow. What validation for me in living my truth! I may have needed a little jump start, but when I really thought about it, I was getting in touch with my own unique purpose – and starting to really hear how other people viewed me, which helped me view myself the same way.

You really do have to have a savage beast inside of you to go out on a limb, rock the boat, follow your heart or any other cliché you can think of when it comes to bringing your whole self to the workplace.

It's crazy to think about being that vulnerable, human, transparent, authentic and real with co-workers and bosses whose job it is to chew you up and spit you out, right? If that is what we expect, we can be sure that's what we will find.

I hold out hope that we're all in desperate search for the workplace that will allow us to be ourselves and use the unique gifts and talents we've been given. Maybe that sounds like Pollyanna, or pie in the sky, or like I'm a hopeless optimist, but someone's got to hold up that end of the argument in order to come to something in the middle.

I had an interesting conversation with a business associate regarding what I termed "love-based" (borrowing from M. Scott Peck's definition of love which relates to cathexis, the extending of one's ego boundaries to include another) vs. fear-based organizations (no definition needed) and whether it is "easier" to work in one or the other. My associate, who was a rather new employee at what we determined was a love-based organization, actually said it was easier to work in a fear-based environment because she knew what to expect. In this new love-based environment, she was expected to be more creative and bring more of herself to work, which caused a lot of trepidation and second-guessing. "How can this be? It seems too good to be true. When is the other shoe going to drop?" were the types of comments she suggested came up for her co-workers.

She shared her belief that even though the management or leadership would like to create a culture of love and support, the individuals involved in the organization still bring their wounds and baggage from other situations into the space, and end up remaining cynical and resigned even though that isn't the intention for the organization.

This was interesting information, because it pointed out that it might not be enough simply to invite the presence of love-based leadership into a culture. Even if we achieve that result, we still need to address the reality of the baggage some choose not to (or don't know how to) get rid of.

It's a brave new world for people who are committed to stepping into the unknown. Our basic humanity would beg us to remain on familiar ground, even though it's no longer comfortable ground. Many of us will choose uncomfortable familiarity over the unknown, even if the unknown will give us more of what we so desperately seek, though we may not be able to successfully articulate what that is within in this new realm.

That's the beauty of taking the plunge, however. There are other brave souls who have made the venture before us and are forging the trail through uncharted territory of love and work. It won't be easy, surely, but what that's significant is easy?

So start thinking about those areas of your life that really make you come alive. What do you absolutely love to do – so much that when you're doing it, time just seems to fly? What is the pleasure you get from doing and being that? What activities or situations do you consistently enjoy doing or giving to others? Make a list of those things and you might be able to see that those activities and situations honor your personal values.

What things cause the hair on the back of your neck to stand up? What causes your shoulders to tense up and your stomach to begin to churn? Instead of getting defensive, try paying attention in a more objective fashion. Maybe those situations or circumstances are incidents where your values were stepped on. Everything can provide a learning opportunity if we can see beyond our initial reactions and be objective about who we really are.

By stepping into your own personal power, you can celebrate your own authentic beingness and support others in doing and being the same for themselves. Live the life you've been blessed with. As Ralph Waldo Emerson said:

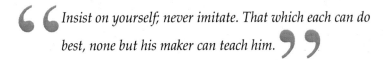

Insist on yourself; never imitate. That which each can do best, none but his maker can teach him.

REALITY CHECKLIST

(complete and repeat as needed)

What does it mean to me to be authentic? _____

_____

_____

_____

_____

What am I doing to be more authentic? _____

_____

_____

_____

_____

How is it working? _____

_____

_____

_____

_____

What might I do differently? _____

_____

_____

_____

_____

The DECISION DILEMMA

"Just do it."

~ Nike corporation

I once heard a quote from Theodore Roosevelt about making decisions. He said that when faced with the need to make a decision, the best thing you can do is make the right decision (surprise). The second best thing is to make the wrong decision. And the worst thing you can do is make no decision.

That makes some sense to me, although it implies that there is a clear-cut "right" and "wrong," which isn't always the case. However, if you make what you consider to be the "wrong" decision, at least you can move toward making a different one much more quickly than if you're in the "ready – aim – aim – aim – aim ..." mode. The true value is in learning something no matter what you decide.

The word "decide" is an interesting word – the root of which is the same as homicide, genocide, suicide. "Decide," in this way, refers to the killing off of other options.

So often it seems the most difficult thing for people to do when they need to make a decision is to take responsibility and do something. There is a huge gap between what we know and what we do. The knowledge we gain from reading or talking with someone else is only as effective as our action.

Perhaps the reason we're afraid to make a decision is because we're living in expectation or holding ourselves to our past experiences where things didn't turn out and we blamed ourselves for making the wrong decision.

You've probably heard the story about putting fleas in a jar with a lid on it. The fleas will jump as high as they can, hitting their heads on the lid. After a while, they will get tired of hitting their heads on the lid, and will start jumping just high enough to avoid the headache. If you take off the lid, they'll only jump as high as they've been conditioned to jump before hitting their heads, even though they are now free to jump as high as they'd like.

We're conditioned, too. We've *decided* that our lives are as they are. We sit in blame and wallow in our own self pity. We don't want to know any more information than we have to support our comfortable – and familiar – existence.

But sometimes something happens to knock us out of our familiarity. Often it is a tragedy, or some other rude awakening. We resist and what we resist persists. We get more awareness, but we fight it, and turn to anger instead.

We know the old way isn't working anymore, but we don't want to be responsible to make a decision on our own. So we don't. We search desperately for a different answer than the one that will force us to change something.

We ask others how, and if we don't like that answer, we ask someone else. Anything to avoid making a decision on our own.

When we really think about it though, it's much easier in the big picture to get to that point where we're acting on our own decisions. Oliver Wendell Holmes said "I wouldn't give a fig for the simplicity on this side of complexity, but I would give my right arm for the simplicity on the far side of complexity."

It seems difficult now, on this side of complexity, but once we make that decision, we can't look back. Once we've "killed off" the other options, we can go ahead and take the action we need to take.

Ah, but there's the rub. It's not enough simply to decide, we need to act.

I train new supervisors in manufacturing environments on a program called Job Relations. It's one part of a three-part training session developed by the U.S. government during World War II to keep production up when our workers went to war. The U.S. government had to get new workers up to speed quickly, so developed quick and easy 4-step methods for doing that. Job Relations trains these supervisors how to solve people problems and to set the foundations for good relations in order to help alleviate some of the problems.

The four steps of this method, 1) Get the Facts, 2) Weigh and Decide, 3) Take Action, and 4) Check Results, is a great model for anyone to use for any type of problem. Notice that the second step is very concerned with taking the time to weigh the facts before making the decision. That's the "aim" in the "ready-aim-fire" model. The third step, then, is to pull the trigger – to actually take the action. Following up ensures us the results we intended – or gives us a chance to redirect our action.

I like John Boyd's decision-making model. Boyd was a fighter pilot in the 1950s. His relentless pursuit of success helped him create his own decision-making model which has come to be known as the OODA Loop. "OODA" is an acronym for the steps in the process: Observe – Orient – Decide – Act. Boyd's idea was to get the loop spinning as fast as necessary to make the decision that garners the outcome you want. The first decision may not be the best, so you just observe, reorient, decide a new route and act.

Another concept to think about when faced with a decision is to consider Robert K. Cooper's idea from *The Other 90%* where he claims we have three brains in our bodies: the head brain, the heart brain and the gut brain. In the past, especially in business, I had let my head brain rule, despite what my heart and my gut were saying.

As an externally focused business person and athlete, I tended to be more concerned with what others thought of me than what I might have really thought was true for me. Consequently, I made decisions based not on what reflected my truth, but on what my head brain told me would be "the right answer" based on others' views. Perhaps part of the problem for me at that point was my lack of confidence in my own knowing because it tended to contradict what others around me believed to be "right."

Again with the benefit of hindsight, had I listened more to the other two brains, I may have been able to make a better decision more quickly, but I may not have gotten the same lesson from the experience that I am able to see myself having learned.

It's really pretty simple to get beyond any guilt or shame I might still have for making less-than-wise decisions in the past. All I need to tell myself now is "I just didn't know then – but now I do. So what am I committed to do to make different decisions in the future?"

There are several models available to assist in ethical decision making, and most of them have something to do with shared or core values. The most difficult decisions usually aren't those between right and wrong, but between right and right. When faced with two equally valuable choices, neither of which conflicts with shared or core values, here are some suggested questions that can be used to narrow the choices.

- **Is it Just?**
  Will you be violating any criminal laws, civil laws, or policies by making this decision?

- **Will it Build Good Will and Positive Relationships?**
  Is it fair to all of the people involved both in the short-term and in the long-term? Will your decision create a win-win situation for those involved?

- **Is it "Right"?**
  How does this decision make you feel about yourself? What do your head, heart, and gut tell you about the decision? Would you like others to know you made the decision you did?

Making decisions is a skill to be practiced and perfected, but it can't end with making the decisions. The proof is in the pudding. The actions will speak much more loudly than the words. Commit to using some method, whether it's the Job Relations model, the above questions, or something else that will work best for you. Don't just talk about doing something—decide what to do and then actually do it.

REALITY CHECKLIST

(complete and repeat as needed)

How do I typically make decisions? Ready—Aim—Fire? Ready—Aim—Aim—Aim ...? Or Ready—Fire—Aim? _____

_____

_____

_____

_____

_____

_____

_____

_____

How is it working? _____

_____

_____

_____

_____

What might I do differently? _____

_____

_____

_____

_____

The COMMUNICATION COMPLICATION

"If you can't say anything nice, don't say anything at all."

~ Your Mother

We've all learned throughout our lives from one teacher or another – even a parent or grandparent somewhere – the quote that opens this chapter, right? There is something to be said for being courteous and polite. But to withhold communication because you don't think what you have to say is nice? Come on. How nice is it not to tell someone they have broccoli in their teeth?

Many of us tend to rely on our pasts to keep us right smack dab where we find ourselves today ... and have lots of good reasons and excuses for staying put.

The best way I know of to get beyond "nice" is to be authentic and honest. Sometimes that means telling someone the truth when they ask what you think about their new haircut. Or when they ask you for feedback on yesterday's board presentation. If given the opportunity to provide an honest opinion, some of us believe that that honest feedback might not be nice - and we end up withholding valuable information from our colleagues or significant others, which keeps them in the same place, doing the same thing over and over, wondering why people aren't responding in a different manner.

Of course, this is a process. Our subconscious conditioning – that little voice in our minds that is always chattering – is almost always critical, judgmental, and, for the most part, negative. So if that little voice is running the show in your mind, then what comes out of your mouth probably matches those thoughts. In that case, it is better to keep your mouth shut than to just react to that voice.

With all of the seemingly controversial topics in the universe, it's a wonder we ever come to any kind of agreement or understanding. I even struggled with which words to use here as any term I might use for "communication" has a distinct meaning, put there either by the dictionary definition or by our past experiences.

Whenever there are opportunities for conversations, there will also be challenges. We may find ourselves in one of two types of situations: 1) one where most everyone agrees (or appears to agree to avoid "conflict"), or 2) one where there are definite "sides" and there doesn't appear to be much learning intent present.

If the outcome of our communication comes down to intention, it's probably no wonder that we tend to avoid these critical conversations. We struggle with what we really want in so many areas of our lives. So why should it be surprising that we would struggle with accepting ideas that are different from our own, when in many cases we haven't really examined our own beliefs at a more than superficial level?

Many people appear to have adopted their beliefs, values, worldviews, political and religious affiliations through their upbringing - and often have seen very little need to go beyond what they believe to be true through their original conditioning or programming. Do you remember when you were a little kid and had a sneaking suspicion that it was your dad who was putting candy in your Christmas stocking and not the actual jolly bearded guy? I remember that thought popping up when I was little, but if I didn't think about it too much, then I didn't have to accept the truth. I could keep my belief, even though I knew better.

But there came a time in my own life – I'm sure there does in everyone's life – when I had to accept the fact that Santa was a legend and didn't really come down the chimney on Christmas Eve to deliver presents to all the good boys and girls. At that point I had to re-think my belief system and go with what I really knew to be true, despite what I may have wanted to hold onto.

So what is the catalyst that causes humans to re-examine previously held beliefs? Does every human being come to that point sometime where old beliefs and worldviews just don't work anymore or are there some people who just go along without ever questioning their own intuition?

As an English major, I'm very interested in the words we choose to use regarding our communication. There are probably many times we don't even know the real definitions of the words we use, and may be stuck in our own understanding of those words. Consider the word discussion, for example. This word has the same Greek root as percussion and concussion, which could come to mean, then, that I have an idea and I'm going to make sure it gets across. We probably have used that word interchangeably with the word dialogue, which implies that the participants suspend their own assumptions for the purpose of learning something.

If we're not open to learning, we won't get beyond the meanings we've assigned based mostly on our own individual experiences.

What is our intention as we come to a situation where information can be exchanged with another? Is there hope in coming to some sort of shared experience through our communication? Can we suspend our own beliefs long enough to learn something from someone with whom we disagree?

Maybe I'm an eternal optimist, but I sure hope so. If we mindfully engage in a dialogue, we might come right back to our original belief, but at least we can be more certain that that belief is true for us if we've tested it against something different.

So unless we are open to dialogue, using this definition, can we really ever achieve more than a cursory understanding of another point of view? Are we merely going through the motions when discussing topics like politics or religion? Instead of polarizing our relationships, might there be an opportunity to build shared meaning by suspending our own assumptions?

How important is intention? I see that the most effective way to add to that shared meaning in communication is to make our intention one of total suspension of preconceived ideas. Otherwise everyone brings expectations which can cloud the opportunity for learning.

I'm reminded of Daniel Quinn's *Thoughts on Dialogue* in which he says that "People who are always learning are always ready to engage in dialogue. People who feel they already know everything or who are afraid to learn cannot engage in dialogue."

If we can figure out how to be authentic in our conversations, and how to really be present and listen, we can be better salespeople, bosses, colleagues, coaches, siblings, parents, in short, better people.

Perhaps the most amazing insight I've had recently regarding my own communication is that rarely do I shut my mouth long enough to learn from others.

In addition to my English major, I also majored in communications, so I should be really good at communicating, right? Where along the way did I miss the class on active listening? Maybe that's what they mean when they say that you teach what you most need to learn. I'm interested in communication and have dedicated my career to supporting people in more effective communication because I need to learn it myself.

One thing I do remember learning was that in order to be the most effective in our communication efforts, it is important to know about the three channels through which our messages are delivered: the visual – what we see; the vocal – what we hear; and the verbal – the actual words we use. Research has shown that 55% of the total communication is the visual; 38% is the vocal; and just 7% is the actual words used. By understanding these distinctions, we have a great opportunity to make sure we all are speaking the same message.

Although research has proven those three V's in communication, I'm beginning to wonder if we shouldn't add a fourth V: visceral. That would represent the feeling or energy you sense from the communication. When we are clear about our intent, it really can override any of the other channels. For example, many people hate going to hospitals to visit sick friends or relatives. It's not the relatives they hate, it's the idea of the hospital, for whatever reason. We're worried about what we will say. But if our intent – our visceral channel of the communication – is loving and supportive, we won't even have to worry about the words (verbal). In fact, just showing up is 55% of the communication (visual). Visceral can interfere with visual, too – as intent will show through loud and clear in the visual.

My dad was a big guy with a big heart, but didn't have a whole lot to say, in many cases. And when he died, I had a chance to be on the receiving end of that awkward "I don't know what to say" conversation everyone experiences in those kinds of situations. There were so many people who came to my mom's house that week following his death who really showed their love and support. I remember most that they were there; I don't remember exactly what they said. What I realized then is really true: the words don't matter nearly as much as just showing up.

Since that time, I've become more interested in what I can learn about my own communication by observing others. When I have been able to consciously take myself out of conversation situations and just watch, I have become amazed at how much I can and do learn when I just shut my mouth.

There was a time I was involved in a book club which I thought was intended to be a dialogue where people suspend their assumptions for the purpose of learning and sharing meaning. But as it turned into what I perceived to be a discussion instead of a dialogue, I started thinking about what I was observing in a new way.

I'm wondering if as businesspeople we ever have opportunities in our daily lives to be in situations where we can participate in dialogue. Where in our work lives are assumptions suspended for the good of the whole? I can't think of too many examples off the top of my head. When in family lives does this realistically happen? How about in community organizations?

We've been forced into situations where we have to fight to be heard. If we don't ram our ideas in there, we'll be lost in the shuffle. So even if we had declared our book club to be a dialogue, this might have been the only place people had been allowed to participate at that level, with most of their previous experience having been in discussion mode.

My book club experience reminded me that even in truly supportive situations, many people are waiting for the other shoe to drop. They've been conditioned by past experiences to bring their baggage with them. Even in new surroundings, many people still act as if they're in familiar territory. Is it any wonder they would be hesitant to trust a new group? When have they had a chance to practice?

In addition to that earlier book study group, I've had the fortune to have been involved in facilitating master mind groups studying the classic book *Think and Grow Rich!* where groups of people gather with like-minded individuals to share goals and dreams, and to hold space for each other to accomplish those goals. One of the unexpected benefits I've received from the members of these groups is ongoing support in developing my own communication skills – both interpersonally and intrapersonally.

These groups have come together for the express purpose of learning and growing together, and some have even created specific and stated intentions for their time together. We find that by stating that intention at the start, we live into that future, and get a chance to practice open and honest dialogue as opposed to the fear-based discussion mode that may come from previous experience.

Of course the second part of effective communication is listening. But, as stated earlier, when are we ever taught how to listen?

It's amazing how powerful speakers can become when listeners hold space for them to be powerful just by the way they listen. Each time I deliver a keynote speech or present material to a client, I'm only as effective as they allow me to be by their listening.

Powerful listening is powerful even in a one-on-one conversation. Try suspending all judgment and opening up a space for someone the next time you have an opportunity. I'm betting you'll be amazed at what you hear!

We all know what happens to us physically when someone tells us what we have to do, or what we should do, or that we're doing something wrong, or any number of other statements that we don't want to hear. Our defenses come up and we end up debating rather than communicating.

I'm starting to discover - finally – that a reason people have so much trouble with effective communication might have a lot to do with biology.

People respond to anything they don't know with defensiveness. It becomes a physical response. You can see it in their posture and the set of their jaw. And it all goes back to that reptilian brain way inside our heads (see more about this in a previous chapter about fear).

That part of our brain has a fight-or-flight response to anything new or unexpected. This brain reaction makes us rigid, obsessive, compulsive and paranoid. It is the part of our brain that keeps repeating past behaviors, and doesn't learn from them.

Thankfully we do have two other more evolved brains in our heads that make us more human and highly developed. So why is it that the smallest and most primitive portion of our brain is often the one that takes over? Shouldn't we be able to override that instinct with our intellect?

Is it any wonder we humans get defensive in our communication style when faced with new information or unfamiliar subject matter or, worse yet, new emotional ground? We don't know how to listen because we're too busy defending. We're in survival mode and we don't know any better because we haven't practiced anything else.

What if you changed the rules for yourself and didn't get defensive when you heard something that went against your initial beliefs? What if you changed the rules of your game and didn't make it wrong that people get defensive?

Everything that comes into our awareness brings with it a lesson for us. And often those lessons that are the most valuable are those that bring the most upset. After all, what better way to notice our progress than by noticing that we have become much more peaceful and effective in our communication?

The good news is that we're humans, not reptiles. We have every opportunity and every responsibility to let the more human parts of our brain in on our communication. What if, as Jerry Hirschberg of the Nissan Corporation once said, we fight the 2 D's in our communication (Defensiveness and Debating) with the 2 L's (Listening and Learning)?

I'm confident that noticing which of our brains is responding to new information in a communication setting will start alerting us to new, more effective habits in our behaviors. As we notice results from these new behaviors, we will be setting the stage for more effective communication in all areas of our lives, and supporting others in doing the same.

REALITY CHECKLIST

(complete and repeat as needed)

What do I know about my communication style (both speaking and listening)? What effect does my communication style have on those around me? _____

_____

_____

_____

What am I doing to get a different perspective? _____

_____

_____

_____

How is it working? _____

_____

_____

_____

_____

What might I do differently? _____

_____

_____

_____

The 100% FACTOR

"There are no such things as limits to growth, because there are no limits on the human capacity for intelligence, imagination and wonder."

~ Ronald Reagan

If you're reading this book, you have at least one thing in common with your fellow readers – your humanity. Simply by virtue of your being human, you have the capacity to do *anything* any other human being can do – anything from discovering new planets to annihilating an entire class of people. We can learn any language known to humankind, and probably other skills not even invented yet. Our capacity is virtually unlimited. So the challenge we have is not with the capacity. It's with moving beyond the possibility to the application.

The first challenge is understanding capacity. Do we believe that our capacity is unlimited? Do we really believe that anything any human being could do, be, or become is available to any of us? If we don't believe that, we can't really move on to a more advanced conversation.

Theoretical psychologist Carl Jung talked about capacity in a slightly different way, using shadow imagery. I first heard about the shadow side of humanity from Rosanne Bane, author of *Dancing in the Dragons Den* – and have since heard a lot about this concept from other sources.

What I remember most about Rosanne Bane's conversation was that as we try to hide or deny those thoughts or feelings that would be considered "shadow" thoughts – the less-than-positive attributes available to all humans – it's like trying to hold an inflated beach ball under water. It's possible to do that for a while, but eventually the ball pops up out of the water and hits us in the face.

The purpose of this chapter is not to rehash the work that has been done by other people. For me it's enough to believe that it is true that our capacity for living amazingly full and fulfilled lives is limited only by the constraints we put upon ourselves.

If we can accept that fact, we can move on to talk more about developing our capacity. As adults our perceived capacity for learning has been stunted by our life experiences. We make choices based on what we've learned by having things work out or not work out, and we determine our own capacity in a certain area.

The statement "I'll never be good at math because my dad told me I couldn't subtract my way out of a paper bag" allows us to live a diminished capacity in the area of math skills. Comparing ourselves to others causes us to live in others' viewpoints instead of looking inside ourselves to develop our own capacity.

"Developing our capacity" implies that we are already limited in our possibilities. If this is the case, we may have to taste some success before we can return to the belief that our capacity is unlimited in all areas. In this case, we may want to play around with the 100% factor.

When something is full, we say it is at maximum capacity. A 20-ounce bottle of soda can only hold 20 ounces – that is its maximum capacity. If we try to pour more than 20 ounces of soda into that bottle, it will overflow.

Yet a one-ounce shot glass that is full is also at maximum capacity – 100% - even though it only holds one ounce. One hundred percent is still 100%. Instead of beating ourselves up about not being a gallon jug in a certain area of our lives, what if we altered the size of our vessel in that certain area in order to give 100%?

Building our capacity is similar to building our muscles or learning a new skill. It takes practice. These might include areas like the capacity to feel, the capacity to understand, the capacity to relate, or something as tangible as the capacity to swim underwater longer (lung capacity), or ability to make money (earning capacity).

As with anything new, expanding our capacity in any area involves a commitment to building something over time. As we overcome the fears which may have limited us in the past, we find it easier to take on new challenges. And perhaps the most exciting aspect of building capacity is our own ability to alter our perspective by visualizing the size of the vessel in various areas where we'd like to make a difference.

There is a challenge to examining our capacity, especially for those of us who are competitive by nature. Sometimes this competitiveness shows up as a chance to give even more than 100%. That was true in my own life as an All-American basketball player, and also as a driven, Type-A businessperson. In those types of endeavors that competitive spirit served me well: I was on several winning teams and also won my share of awards in the business world, all the externals one would expect for stellar performance.

However, comparing my percentage to others, while offering me a chance to prove that I was "better than" someone else, seemed most often to leave me with a level of stress and anxiety that I couldn't always identify. I've since come to realize that if I'm living authentically and am being my best creative self, there really is no competition because nobody can bring the unique set of strengths that is mine and mine alone.

Overflowing your current container can often leave you feeling as unfulfilled as living a half-full existence if both experiences highlight what's not working rather than what is working.

That's why it's so important to determine what maximum capacity feels like, regardless of the task or endeavor. Try a new task with the intention of learning something new, giving up your attachment to what "success" might look like on the outside or what it might look like to someone else.

I sing in a barbershop chorus, and there used to be a time when our director would ask us, after we'd rehearsed a song from front to back, "how many of you feel that was the best performance you've ever given?" Very rarely did any hands go up. Why not? What were we waiting for? If we weren't giving the best performance of our lives – up to that point – what was the point?

As a chorus we've since begun to discover what our own personal 100% feels like, and we're much more likely to practice in that new space, which makes our overall performance much more satisfying. When we know we're operating at our maximum capacity as a unit, the external validation and scoring really doesn't matter as much as it used to when we were singing to pursue that goal. And the irony is that as we've given up that attachment, the external validation follows.

We've all heard the stories of people who took on a new hobby like painting late in life when others might have thought it was too late, only to achieve greatness by starting small. Slow and steady wins the race, we learn from Aesop's fable of the tortoise and the hare.

Of course, there may be times when you're not able to give 100%. What if you're in the middle of a task and you realize your maximum capacity is 40% at that moment? One thing that has really helped me in the past is to rely on what I call my posse. These are the people in my life who I know will be honest with me when I'm not able to be objective. Since we've all agreed that we want to build our individual and collective capacity, we have a much broader perspective and give each other permission to say it like it is.

When things get frantic and frenzied for you, you might also consider a new mental perspective. Imagine yourself in a hot-air balloon tethered 50 feet above your situation where you have an opportunity to watch yourself instead of being in the middle of the situation. Or think about how you would view your life as a sitcom or a theatrical production. How does the person playing your character in the drama or comedy act or react to situations? How do the supporting characters respond to your actions (because after all, you are the star!)? If you give yourself the opportunity to see the drama from a different perspective, you'll often find that what you're doing with all the "stuff" in your life is actually more of a comedy than you might think when you're in the thick of it.

Which brings up yet another distinction in *The 100% Factor*: the distinction between what we're doing and what we're being. If we look at maximum capacity only through the eyes of what we're doing to achieve results, we're missing a whole new dimension of 100%.

As I've said earlier, in my corporate career – and in my former life as an athlete – I was conditioned to believe that success was measured by others out there. Corporate awards and athletic endeavors where there was a winner and a loser afforded me a chance to measure results in a way the external world validated.

Even the barbershop chorus and quartet I sing with participate in a competition each spring to measure progress by earning points in comparison to the other choruses or quartets. There was a time in my chorus life where I just didn't understand that the "doing" part of singing isn't where the real satisfaction comes from. What I'm learning today is that it's the "being" that provides me the most long-lasting and fulfilling intrinsic rewards.

Shakespeare really had a great perspective on the distinction between "doing" and "being" as he relayed in Hamlet's familiar monologue:

> *To be, or not to be: that is the question:*
> *Whether 'tis nobler in the mind to suffer*
> *the slings and arrows of outrageous fortune,*
> *Or to take arms against a sea of troubles,*
> *And by opposing end them.*

Is it better to *be* in the mind or to take arms and do something? I think there's a time and a place for both ... the question really is when to do and when to be.

Lance Secretan has a similar idea in his book *Inspire*. He calls it the Why-Be-Do model and this makes so much sense to me as a Life Purpose and Career Coach.

He says it's about Destiny (WHY am I here) which leads us to Cause (How will I BE - what will I stand for) which leads us to Calling (What will I DO). When we get that figured out, we might consider rethinking our need to HAVE things in order to DO more in order to BE happy.

One way to practice maximizing your own capacity is to start noticing your breathing. Taking a deeper breath when you think about it will allow you to DO something that yields more BEING.

When you get familiar with the feeling of excellence and mastery instead of the stress associated with not being full enough (taking on a container that's too big) or the disappointment and resentment that can come with being too full (resisting moving to a bigger container), you will know better when it's time to take on a new container instead of blaming the one in which you find yourself.

That level of 100% is a great indicator of living fully because it allows just enough challenge to keep things exciting, but doesn't overwhelm you enough to quit. It's a very personal level, however, and one that will be different for everyone.

But getting familiar with your own capacity and being committed to living at 100% will give you joy and fulfillment beyond compare. Give it a try. What do you have to lose?

REALITY CHECKLIST

(complete and repeat as needed)

What do I believe about my own capacity? _____

_____

_____

_____

_____

*What am I doing to increase my capacity, and in which areas of my life am I
concentrating that capacity?* _____

_____

_____

_____

How is it working? _____

_____

_____

_____

_____

What might I do differently? _____

_____

_____

_____

_____

The PROBLEM WITH KNOWLEDGE

"You know more than you think."

~ Your college philosophy professor

Ignorance really is bliss, isn't it? When we don't know anything about a topic, how can we possibly be responsible for anything related to that topic? But, as Oliver Wendell Holmes said, "A man's mind, once expanded by a new thought, cannot regain its original dimensions." Once you gain some knowledge about a particular area, it's likely that you will want to do things differently as a result of that knowledge.

There is a distinction between knowledge and skill. Knowledge is what you learn from reading books or from experience. Knowledge is in your head. Skill is what you do with the knowledge to get it from your head to your hands and into the world.

It's pretty difficult to go from knowledge to competence without a stopover in the skill area. I'm sure there are some people who can read about playing the piano and then sit down and play a concerto without practicing, but I'm betting they are much rarer than those of us who need to practice to perfect our skills.

My mom used to tell me during all those years of piano lessons that practice makes perfect. So in order to perfect my piano playing, I needed to practice. I learned, however, through that experience, that practice makes permanent – the way you practice will dictate the way you will perform. Since I wasn't all that keen about perfect practice, the result of my 12 years of piano lessons is much less than perfect performance.

So consider the knowledge you already have. You probably *know* more than you *think* you know ... or you know more than you think – you just may not take the time to think about it.

Why are we so compelled to take our opinions from others? We are conditioned early in our lives not to trust our own beliefs; not to trust our own knowingness. Our belief system is handed to us from our parents, our siblings, our friends, teachers, co-workers, bosses – nearly everyone else we come into contact with. But there may come a time in our lives when our beliefs conflict with our knowingness.

Does trusting our own knowingness come with age? With wisdom? With experience? If so, is there anything that young people really can know without having experienced it themselves?

If so, where is that point at which we know? When we're 20? 30? 50? 80?

I'm all about connecting with our inner knowing. Maybe it starts with defining that inner knowing - the collection of all the wisdom we've accumulated over the years and either discounted because it didn't fit with who we were or accepted because it did. I wonder if we get to a point in our lives that we've accumulated enough inner wisdom - a critical mass, maybe - that makes it easier to trust both *what* we know and *that* we know.

Wayne Dyer talks about the distinction between what we *believe* and what we *know*. He says that *beliefs* are external; they are given to us throughout our entire lives. They may or may not coincide with what we *know*, which is internal and comes from our soul.

Perhaps you were raised in a family that was Catholic and Democrat and loved the Yankees. Is it just understood that, like everyone else in your family, you, too, will be a Catholic Democrat who loves the Yankees? There's certainly nothing wrong with that, but if you believe those things just because everyone else in your family did, then you're taking your opinions from others without listening to your own inner knowing about what fits you.

I played basketball in college, and as the only freshman on the team that first year I was pretty impressionable. After all, what did I really know about college basketball? The seniors on the team made it clear to me in no uncertain terms that our team hated a particular rival team. I remember wondering in my head why we would hate another group of players, but it became evident very quickly that that was something I was not to question. It just was. It just was that way for me that first year; however, as I got older and more mature, I was able to determine for myself how I felt about any of our rivals. And to this day I've maintained contact with the coach and some of the players of that particular "rival" team.

I've questioned unexplained beliefs and blind faith as far back as I can remember. I've always been a questioner, as you can read in the chapter in this book about skepticism. But in my experience, overcoming that initial doubt has produced very strong faith. When I have a chance to make up my mind about something that might be outside the realm of the expected, I find I'm much more connected and centered when I've trusted my own truth.

It's interesting how often – and in how many different contexts - in our English language we use the word "mind." We use it as both a noun and a verb. We tell our children to mind their manners and mind their mothers. What we may not realize is that when we say those things, we really are asking ourselves and others to connect more with our *knowing*. As we change our minds, we create the possibility of changing our lives.

Sometimes we confuse our mind – the part of us we can't see or touch or measure – with our brain, which is tangible. In reality our mind represents our spirit or our inner knowing. Our body – the parts of us that we can see and touch – represents our ego. We have a chance to change our minds to connect with who we really know ourselves to be.

There comes a point in everyone's life - Lance Secretan in the book Inspire! says that sometimes it happens on people's deathbeds, but it does happen - when they connect with their destiny, when the switch flips and they realize what it is they were meant to do with their lives, and also that they can/could have had a life they love.

I don't want to wait until my deathbed, and I'm learning every day - every minute. Yes, as the Beatles tell us, "Living is easy with eyes closed, misunderstanding all you see/It's getting hard to be someone but it all works out, it doesn't matter much to me" (from *Strawberry Fields Forever*).

Don't let fear of the unknown keep you from living with eyes open, learning to understand all you see. It's a much more enlightening place to live as you figure out your own, personalized approach to life!

REALITY CHECKLIST

(complete and repeat as needed)

*What do I **know**? Which parts may have come from other people?* _____

_____

_____

_____

_____

What am I doing to get from beliefs to knowledge to action? _____

_____

_____

_____

_____

How is it working? _____

_____

_____

_____

What might I do differently? _____

_____

_____

_____

The RELATIONSHIP PREDICAMENT

"In business it's not about closing the sale, it's about opening the relationship."

~ Jim Cathcart

I learned something in my career that took me way too long to apply. I was not a business major in college – in fact, it wasn't until I got my master's degree in business management through an accelerated program as an adult that I had any true business education. That is, if you don't count the school of hard knocks.

I think at some gut level I knew that the success of any business depends upon the quality of the relationships within that endeavor. But I had never been taught that through my formal education. When I began my business life, I was book smart, but worldly naïve.

Two of my former bosses taught me some important lessons about the importance of relationships in business. One of them taught me that if it wasn't his idea, it couldn't be valuable. Through his example, he showed that the relationships he found most effective in his life were the relationships that could get him something, not those in which he gave something first. He seemed to feel compelled to drop names whenever he could, and would be able to tell you everything about someone he had seen in an airport as if they were good friends. It is evident now, from a new perspective, that his insecurities about his own self-worth forced him to take this stance with the employees he was managing so he could prove his worth – first to others, and then, hopefully, to himself.

Another of those bosses taught me what not to do in the world of relationships. It wasn't through his actions alone but even through his words that I learned his philosophy about relationship building. He told me that he believed the work I was committed to doing in building relationships with our business partners and vendors, along with the leadership and communication training I was providing, was "touchy feely crap that makes me puke." The last straw that caused me to rethink my employment with his organization was his comment: "Business has nothing to do with relationships."

Marcus Buckingham and Curt Coffman, in their book *First Break All The Rules* said that people leave their work environments not because of the work itself but because of the relationship with their immediate supervisors. My two bosses evidently misunderstood their roles as keepers of the relationship within the organizations.

But I've also grown to understand much more about myself thanks to my own relationships with these bosses. Each of them had so much to teach me about myself, things I'm sure they didn't even realize they were teaching me. It has taken me some time to understand, and to accept, that the only thing those two bosses had in common – along with the two other bosses I had prior to my experiences with them – was me. It was my attitude and my inability to see beyond my victim mentality that kept me stuck in blame mode even after leaving those work environments.

It is only now, in hindsight and in retrospect, that I can see the huge gifts these bosses gave to me. I'm grateful to them for being the messengers for a lesson in trusting my own knowing and listening to my Higher Self.

The relationships I've developed since working for these two bosses have given me access to entirely new ways of doing business. Through these new relationships, I've become interested in opportunities to judge performance success in four different ways, using people's brain preferences.

I have had the great privilege to work with a fabulous company called SolutionPeople (www.solutionpeople.com) where I was first introduced to Ned Herrmann, and his whole-brain research.

According to the article "How to Get More ROI: Return on Intelligence" at the Ned Herrmann website (see www.hbdi.com), people's successful performance can be measured using purpose, process, people, and possibilities. Ideally we all want:

1) Revenue growth/profitability

2) To achieve plans and goals on schedule

3) Employee and customer satisfaction

4) Good long term strategy and innovative/proactive thinking.

Based on Herrmann's brain research, and using a tool called the *Diversity Game*, we can identify which people prefer "left-brained" activities like purpose and process, and which people prefer "right-brained" activities like possibilities and people.

According to this article, if you "use your head" as you define success, you will put your whole brain to work and maybe find success and performance in places you didn't even recognize!

Jim Cathcart is a public speaker and author of the program *Relationship Selling*™. As the quote that opens this chapter demonstrates, he understands the importance of building relationships in a sales environment. However, I think that quote also shows that selling can go way beyond traditional "sales." When your intention in any interaction has more to do with what you can get (the immediate win), the result may well be a closed sale, but that might be it. When your intention has more to do with what you can do for someone else, the result is more often an opened relationship, which can go way beyond the immediate win.

This is true whether you're a traditional salesperson or whether you're building a relationship with someone you supervise or someone you live with. When you think about it, you're really selling all the time. You sell an idea, a place to have lunch, a movie choice, or a vacation destination. Focusing more on the relationship than on the "win," can yield amazing long-term results.

Touchy-feely? Maybe to some. But research shows that people and organizations that choose to pay attention to the "soft stuff" are starting to find the hard results coming their way in the form of purpose, process, possibilities and people. Oh, and ROI.

REALITY CHECKLIST

(complete and repeat as needed)

How much stock do I put in building and maintaining relationships, whether at work or at home? _____

_____

_____

_____

_____

What am I doing to get the results I want? _____

_____

_____

_____

How is it working? _____

_____

_____

_____

_____

What might I do differently? _____

_____

_____

_____

_____

The PRICE of PREJUDICE

**"All seems infected that the infected spy,
as all looks yellow to the jaundiced eye."**

~ Alexander Pope

I s it possible to live in a world free of prejudice? Or is prejudice – pre-judging – an unfortunate consequence of our humanity? I've been thinking a lot about this issue recently – probably in part because of the impact of the Oscar-winning best picture *Crash*. In this 2004 movie set in Los Angeles, a racially and economically diverse group of people live lives that collide with each other in very unexpected ways. Through their interactions, we as viewers are challenged to get beyond the judgment and our tendency to judge books by their covers.

So as soon as I think of the concept of prejudice, the first thing that comes to my mind is race. I was raised in a small town in southeastern North Dakota, and except for one African American family who moved into – and out of – our community, I was not exposed to anyone of another race until I went to a national basketball camp in Georgia between my junior and senior years of high school.

Even now, although I've traveled around the United States and Europe, I still live in a community in southeastern North Dakota where my Caucasian nationality is in the racial majority.

I met an African American man at a conference I attended in Chicago in 2004 and we've remained in touch and have become good friends via phone and e-mail since then. I visited him in Chicago this past year and he introduced me to the associate pastor of his church. I had been talking to my friend for almost a year and he had even introduced me to his associate pastor over the phone – and I honestly had forgotten that he was African American. It was only when I met his pastor in person that I knew he, too, was African American.

As we got into a really in-depth conversation about the things they wanted to talk about regarding the leadership and vision for the church, it finally came up that race might be an issue at the church. When I told my friend and his pastor that I really don't see them as a color, but rather as individuals, the pastor told me that I have to see him as a man of color, because he sees himself that way. Perception is reality and my perception is that race shouldn't matter – people should see each other as colorless. But that's because I come from my own worldview, and I think everyone should see the world the way I see it. The reality is that where I was born and raised – in North Dakota U.S.A. – I am in the racial majority.

The reality of living in white North Dakota is different for a person of color, whether Native American or African American or

Mexican or Bosnian or any number of other ethnic nationalities.

Maybe it's easy for me as a white person to be idealistic about this; it really doesn't occur to me every day that I'm white. I can only imagine what it must be like for those people in my community who are not white. I've heard stories about them seeing white people clutch their own purses more tightly when they walk by, or getting less than excellent service in restaurants. The way they experience the world is very different than the way I experience it and that is their reality. For me to discount it by denying that it is true would be to see the world through my own lens and to expect others to see it that way as well.

I have another friend who was born in an Eastern European country and has offered me yet another viewpoint to consider. Although her skin is pretty much the same color as mine, she has dark eyes and dark hair, and a pronounced accent. She told me that she used to experience similar behavior; most notably attracting a lot of attention by security guards at department stores.

She said that she has made a point to put herself in the shoes of the security guard, and to try to imagine what that person must be going through, being fearful of anyone who looks different. She said she has made a conscious effort to be open about her understanding of being a minority in the community. Since she has made that adjustment for herself, she finds that people are much more open to learning more about her viewpoint and her culture – and they don't follow her as closely in stores anymore. Her perception has actually become her own reality.

As I think more about prejudice, I see that there are other categories around which people could form varied opinions. Race is surely one, but the other obvious category is gender. These are obvious categories because they are external.

What does it mean to be in the majority as it relates to gender? If it's the category with the greatest number, according to the U.S. census, I would be in the majority there, too. Or is the majority in the category of gender the group with the loudest voice?

When we get beyond the obvious categories – the external, observable ones - we find that there are so many categories in which we could form judgments. Political affiliation, career classification, religious affiliation, sexual orientation, height, weight – these are just a few of the many.

Is there ever a chance for humans to get beyond their pre-judging? Or is it just the way it is? Can we hope to see beyond the boundaries that keep us separated? We talk about the word diversity and call it a good thing; yet the root of the very word "Diversity" is "division." We focus much more on the ways we as humans are different than on the ways we are similar.

As a coach, I do my best to be an objective observer and reflect what I hear my clients saying in order to support them in achieving the goals they set for themselves. However, I find that even the observations I choose to comment on automatically have my own judgments involved. Why else would I choose to comment?

I find notice similar observations as I facilitate planning sessions or other client dialogues which require me to record participant comments on a flipchart or white board for everyone to observe. I sometimes catch myself abbreviating their comments to save writing time. My intention is not to judge their comments, but it could certainly appear that way.

So how might we be able to get beyond what keeps us stuck in our own biases? I've heard it said that the only way to stop a game is to stop. Perhaps it will take someone getting tired enough of the game to just stop. Rosa Parks is a great example of someone who just got tired and, on that one fateful day, she didn't give up her seat on the bus. We may think it was an act of defiance on her part that caused the civil rights movement, but she had actually been involved in that movement for 12 years before that day. She was involved because her husband got her involved. And he was involved because someone else got him involved. Rosa's action caused Martin Luther King Jr. to rise to prominence in the movement, but it actually took her stopping the fight to have the real change enacted.

I wonder if her experience as a racial minority might apply to others' experience as minorities in any of the other categories of bias that exist. If the only way to stop something is to stop, perhaps we are making it too difficult.

It is actually really simple to quit something. Just quit. Take smoking, for example. It's much more difficult to smoke. You have to carry matches or a lighter with you at all times, or be able to find a light somewhere. You have to worry about what to do with the ashes. You have to be thinking about what to do with the leftover butts. You have to think about carrying breath mints so your breath doesn't smell like smoke if you're on your way to a meeting. You have to use whitening toothpaste so your teeth don't get discolored. Somewhere in the back of your mind you've got to be thinking about what this might be doing to your long-term health. You have to consider how much it costs to smoke and how much more your health insurance costs because you are a smoker.

It may be simple to quit – just stop. But it's not that easy, whether we're talking about smoking or judging. If it were easy, far fewer people would be doing either of them.

Lucius Annaeus Seneca, a playwright, orator and author who was born in Spain in 4 BC, said "If you judge, investigate." If you have reason to think of someone differently than you think of yourself, it's a great opportunity for you to initiate a conversation – create a dialogue – to learn something beyond what you currently know.

When you get to that point, you stop seeing the world outside yourself and realize that you just might be the change you've been looking for in the world. As all of us shift our own attitudes and prejudices, we realize that we really are influencing a circle much bigger than we originally intended.

Our actions – and even our very thoughts – affect the way the world occurs to us. By becoming aware of the areas of our own prejudice and bias, we can begin to get beyond the preconceptions we bring to interactions with people who have different worldviews or different life experiences.

In situations where you want to break down another person's preconceptions about you, determine what the other person expects of you and then do the opposite. For example, if you are expected to be closed to new ideas, express an interest in listening to new approaches. If you are expected to be selfish and aggressive, take a non-assertive stance and make a small concession that demonstrates good will and a willingness to cooperate. Make your intention one of relationship building instead of one of perpetuating the other's expectation.

The objective is simply to contradict the negative images people can have of others who are different, and to begin to replace them with more positive images – and more positive outcomes.

That which we resist persists, so the answer is not to fight against behaviors or attitudes or actions we don't like (even those behaviors or attitudes we notice within ourselves). A much more positive – and undeniably effective – strategy is to find that which you are willing to stand for. The energy which comes from a place of affirming a person's essential goodness will allow us to respectfully disagree with a position or an opinion, but not with the person himself.

When it comes right down to it, we humans are much more alike than we are different. Finding that which we can connect with seems to me to be a much more positive strategy than pointing out – and living out – our differences.

REALITY CHECKLIST

(complete and repeat as needed)

How do I demonstrate my prejudices or biases? What do I have judgments about? How did my parents and others teach me about "strangers"?

_____

_____

_____

_____

What am I doing to get a different perspective about bias? _____

_____

_____

_____

How is it working? _____

_____

_____

_____

_____

What might I do differently? _____

_____

_____

_____

_____

The ISSUE of ACCOUNTABILITY

"The ancient Romans had a tradition: whenever one of their engineers constructed an arch, as the capstone was hoisted into place, the engineer assumed accountability for his work in the most profound way possible: he stood under the arch."

~ Michael Armstrong

How many of us are able, or even willing to think about, standing under our own work? How much of a stake do we have in our own lives?

In moments of frustration throughout the early years of my career, one of the statements that found its way into my head more than once was "they just don't get it." From the vantage point within my own head, I began having conversations with these elusive **"they"** groups without their even being present, which only led to more frustration because potential dialogues ended up being one-sided monologues.

In thinking back on those moments of frustration, and being accountable to myself for this idea, I don't think I was ever able to actually articulate who "**they**" were. Whether a social organization or a workgroup or even a family unit, as I began to really delve deep into the source of my frustration, I couldn't really get more specific than that.

Merely working to identify the source of my frustration began to help break it up. The most amazing insight to me was that there really was no "**they**" since I am part of the "**they**" I'd been thinking about.

Even more elusive than the "who are they" question to me now is "what is it that they don't get?"

Of course you would expect that the "**it**" in question would shift depending upon the situation; however, in my moments of clarity (as my focus was shifted squarely upon myself), the indefinable "**it**" usually seemed to grasp similar characteristics.

"**It**" usually came to mean "**me**" (as in "they don't get **me**") or "the source of my frustration" (as in "they don't understand this situation that I can't understand any better than to use this trite pronoun to encompass my unwillingness to take responsibility for my part in the confusion.").

"They just don't get it" really was a copout I used to avoid having to have meaningful conversations with any one of the elusive members of "**they**."

Beginning to accept this responsibility doesn't necessarily guarantee an easy out, but it does provide the beginning of a roadmap for some destination, which, really, is a victory.

I submit that "**they**" really do get something. That's where the real conversation can begin.

All of this talk about personal accountability begs a question: Can you really hold someone else accountable? Or is accountability truly a personal decision?

Of course the most effective leaders are those who practice what they preach. Only when you as the leader are proving that accountability begins with you will you have the best chance at building personal accountability in your work teams or even in those teams you are part of outside of work.

It does take a certain amount of personal awareness for a person to recognize when accountability is lacking in his or her own life. It also takes wisdom and maturity to listen to – and especially to seek out – others' feedback. And it takes courage to take the leap and decide to do something about the areas in which you see improvement opportunities.

Once the issue of *personal* accountability has been addressed, there are better opportunities to build team accountability. In order to have the best results in a team situation, think about creating a universal definition of the term that each team member can own and buy into.

When leaders are committed to determining the definition and then implementing accountability programs, they can expect that employees won't have the need to just go through the motions at work. The leader's positive focus and willingness to "practice what she preaches" will create a culture in which great results can be achieved.

I coached one team client for more than a year. The manager was a big reason for the success of the initiative because of her ability to demonstrate what she wanted the rest of the team to embrace. When we worked together to gain new insights, it was so that the members of the team could bring light first to themselves in order to then move on to, using Stephen Covey's term, their *circles of influence*. We wanted my client's customers to choose my client's business because they knew something was different there, even if they couldn't really define what it was.

That conversation led us to an attempt to define this "**it**" we knew was there, but weren't sure how to define. There was something - some spirit, some energy, some sense of something - that drew members/clients/customers to this place.

As we worked to define this "**it**," it began to feel like looking into a starry sky during a dark night and trying to see individual stars. Have you ever tried to do that? Just as you begin to make out a specific cluster, it eludes your focused gaze and you discover that the best way to take in the galaxy is by looking at it as a whole entity.

We know when "**it**" is there ... and we know when "**it**" isn't. Think about that next time you go to a restaurant. Is there something (besides your favorite dish) that draws you back? What about your favorite clothing store? What about your favorite coffee shop - your doctor - your accountant - your grocery store?

Do we need to have a definition of "**it**" to be able to produce or create "**it**" within a work environment or is it enough just to sense "**it**"?

I'm reminded of David Whyte's definition of soul in *The Heart Aroused: Poetry and the Preservation of the Soul in Corporate America.* Here's his take:

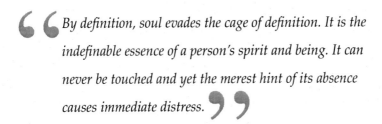 *By definition, soul evades the cage of definition. It is the indefinable essence of a person's spirit and being. It can never be touched and yet the merest hint of its absence causes immediate distress.*

Through my work with this client, I now have a better sense of what "**it**" is. And through the hard work of their staff, I know that, even if they can't pinpoint a definition, their clients know "**it**" because they feel/sense/are surrounded by "**it**" when they're there.

Where in your life is "**it**" missing? Where in your life is "**it**" present? Notice what you notice. Maybe it's not so much about what we can't do in a certain circumstance, but more what we can do. By accepting our own accountability, we will begin to make a difference where we can so that we can influence the people around us by who we are being.

Theodore Roosevelt said it well: "Do what you can, with what you have, where you are."

Indeed.

REALITY CHECKLIST

(complete and repeat as needed)

How do I feel about the whole issue of accountability? _____

_____

_____

_____

_____

What am I doing to become more accountable for things that frustrate me?

_____

_____

_____

_____

How is it working? _____

_____

_____

_____

What might I do differently? _____

_____

_____

_____

The EFFORT EQUATION

"You get out of it what you put into it."

~ Your piano teacher

What context does the word "effort" bring up for you? If you really do get out of a situation what you put into it, does the effort up front yield the results you want? Or is it more work to alter something than to remain the same, even though the long-term effects of a shift up front could produce even more positive results?

When I was growing up in Lisbon, North Dakota, we used to hang out at the park quite a bit. In the middle of the park there was an old pump well, not the free-standing water fountains you see today. I remember it being a contest to see who could get to the pump first, and be the one to struggle with those first few pulls on the handle to get the thing started. Those first pulls were monstrously difficult, but once the water started flowing, it was effortless. And the hard work was so worth it as the ice-cold water flowed into our outstretched hands and splashed onto the cement below. It was really tough to get the water started, but I can't ever remember a time we gave up on those first few difficult strokes because we knew it would get easier and the water would flow.

Isn't it our goal to get to a point where our lives don't have to involve a lot of effort? Don't we want to get to that point where we can take a break and enjoy the fruits of our labor? Are we so conditioned to be in busy mode that we don't know how to relax?

I don't think this business of life is supposed to be a struggle. I don't think it's supposed to be an effort, in the traditional sense. If it's an effort to get up in the morning, get yourself to a boring job, with people who drain your energy, go home, still feeling bored, only to do it all over again the next day, there may be a better way to look at things. There are most certainly new possibilities to create for your life.

We seem to be in a constant state of fix. And we're searching desperately for the quick fix. It's like driving around the parking lot to find a close spot, wasting the time you would have saved if you had just taken a spot and walked.

It's really about time – it's about allowing enough time to let things settle ... to let us see whether our efforts have resulted in the effects we desire. And we need to get beyond the quick fix, which will almost certainly result only in short-term relief, which may lead to even greater pain in the long run.

Doesn't it make more sense to consider why we may be uninspired in our own lives instead of just medicating ourselves to deal with the discomfort? If we will consider the root cause, it will give us a more effective way to determine the effort we want to expend to make the situation different.

Where do you put all of your efforts? Into keeping things the same? Into coming up with reasons why you don't need to take responsibility? Into digging your heels in and resisting?

This might be the way you've looked at effort in the past. As a struggle. As an obligation. As tyranny. You get an A for effort. Is that enough? What matters, the effort or the effect? What is the outcome you want to produce? What are you willing to do to get it?

Think about how you might reframe whatever it is you consider to be effort in your life. My life coach gave me a great analogy to consider when I first started working with her. She told me that when we are born, it's like we are born into this huge mansion, with many rooms and all the toys and gadgets and stuff we could ever imagine having.

But our early childhood and our socialization slowly but surely causes us to shut the doors to the many rooms in the mansion until eventually as adults we are living in a one-room apartment in the midst of everything we could ever want or need.

As my coach, she told me her job was to open some of the doors in my mansion and shine a light into the corners, helping me to remember what I already know but just forgot about who I really am. It may not always be easy, but it's really quite simple.

When you think about it, it is not our job to search for love, for happiness, for abundance, success, or whatever it is that we think is missing in our lives. It is our job to search inside ourselves for the barriers we have placed that prevent us from seeing what is already there.

Have you ever struggled to remember someone's name? Or where you put your car keys? Or what you had for breakfast? We've become very accustomed to that place of struggle. Yet when we just relax and stop trying so hard to remember, in the middle of dinner when we're not even thinking about it, the name will pop into our heads. Or we'll remember where we left the keys – or what the menu was that morning.

Here's an experiment to try. Instead of setting your alarm, just tell yourself, before you go to sleep, what time you want to wake up the next morning. If you sincerely let go of the expectation that it won't work, your body will wake you up without the alarm clock. Try it – but be really clear about intending that it will work and see what you can produce.

Trust that what is already there is worth any effort you have to make up front to yield the results you wish for yourself and your life. Make up your mind to change your mind about effort. Life doesn't have to be a struggle if a positive outcome is already assured. Just make the commitment to pull on the pump handle and the water will flow. Guaranteed.

REALITY CHECKLIST

(complete and repeat as needed)

How do I feel about effort? Why is effort important to me? _____

_____

_____

_____

_____

Where do I tend to concentrate my efforts? _____

_____

_____

_____

_____

How is it working? _____

_____

_____

_____

_____

What might I do differently? _____

_____

_____

_____

_____

The SKEPTIC'S PLAYGROUND

"It'll never work anyway."

— Your Co-Workers

S o, when you read the title of this chapter, did you automatically draw a conclusion in your mind about what a "skeptic" is? Did that word have a negative or a positive connotation in your mind?

We have been conditioned that to have the answers is preferable to having the questions. But we forget that in order to find the answers, we first have to have the questions – and be willing to ask them.

I must admit, when it first occurred to me to write about skepticism, I was thinking about those people who never trust anything unless they have proof; those people who want to live in what they already know, not what might be possible; those people who won't support anything new; people who are basically difficult to have a conversation with because they question the logic of every idea. For me, the word had a negative connotation.

But when I looked up the meaning of the word at dictionary.com, I found out that the definition is:

> *One who instinctively or habitually doubts, questions, or disagrees with assertions or generally accepted conclusions.*

And I discovered that I am a skeptic.

I've always been a questioner. As far back as I can remember, I had to know why things were the way they were, and whether or not they had to be that way. I really don't believe I was trying to be difficult - I was just curious.

But the older I got, the more I began to understand that questions didn't always have answers, and the people to whom I was addressing my questions didn't want to appear uninformed or unintelligent, so they encouraged me to stop asking questions. Whether this was in school, in Sunday school, or even at home, I remember the effect of my questions on my teachers and parents, and I remember that I slowly began to shut up - at least on the outside.

But now I wonder, where would we be in our world of science, religion, education, business without those people who "instinctively doubt, question or disagree with generally accepted conclusions"?

Maybe for me the hang-up has been with the word "habitually" in that definition. Even the "right" thing done for the "wrong" reasons is still "wrong," right?

Was I asking questions all my life just to be difficult? Was it a habit? I don't think so. I'd like to get beyond my own preconceived notions and concepts and trust my own gut and instincts. Maybe that's why I asked other people for the answer - because I didn't trust my own knowing. Maybe I wanted validation. Maybe I wanted to be acknowledged. Maybe I just wanted attention. I'd like to think my reasons for being curious evolved as I evolved throughout my life.

Perhaps people have to be skeptical as they're learning things in their lives. Perhaps it's their conditioning that turns them from intuitive skeptics into habitual skeptics. Let's not let past perceptions - others' or our own - keep us from questioning.

Through my work with SolutionPeople in Chicago I've learned the value of asking questions. One of the benefits of working with this organization is the development of a question bank, specific to whatever goal, challenge or problem the client is working on. This process provides an opportunity for the client to solicit questions from throughout – and outside – their own organizations in order to tackle goals from various angles. The people are not only involved in asking questions of the organization, but also in coming up with potential solutions.

In her book *Change Your Questions, Change Your Life*, Marilee G. Adams, PhD introduces QuestionThinking, which gives a formula for intentionally shifting internal questions to put people in charge of their own thoughts. She says, in the book, that "a world of questions is a world of possibility. Questions open our minds, connect us to each other, and shake outmoded paradigms."

Marilee says that our individual thinking actually occurs as a question and answer process, and she uses the example of selecting something to wear to work. You first have to ask yourself questions about the weather, what's clean, what's comfortable, and maybe even who you'll be meeting with that day. You answer those questions by doing something, in this case, selecting an appropriate outfit.

Asking questions can actually deepen conviction. As Robert Browning said, "I show you doubt to prove that faith exists."

So let's get back out there and be curious. Ask questions. Challenge the status quo. And don't be afraid to look inside yourself for the answers.

REALITY CHECKLIST

(complete and repeat as needed)

Do I ask a lot of questions? In what ways am I a skeptic? _____

_____

_____

_____

_____

What am I doing to question the status quo? _____

_____

_____

_____

_____

How is it working? _____

_____

_____

_____

_____

What might I do differently? _____

_____

_____

_____

_____

The HAZARDS OF PASSION

"There's no crying in baseball."

—Tom Hanks in "A League of Their Own"

P assion is often expressed as emotion, which sometimes intimidates people who want to keep emotions at bay. This seems to be especially true in the workplace. Yet employers often want their employees to bring their 100% - their maximum capacity - to work. What we sometimes forget is that when we want people to bring all of themselves, we have to expect that that will include the "good" as well as the "bad." Passion is passion whether it's happiness or other intensity.

Why are we afraid of emotion? Is it because we don't know what to do when we see people expressing any kind of emotion past dead center? Whether it's laughing or crying, too much of either is still too much.

I'm reminded of the Mary Tyler Moore Show episode where they're at the funeral of Chuckles the Clown, who, while dressed as a peanut, was killed by an elephant. Mary is appalled by the jokes her co-workers are telling around the office about Chuckles' unfortunate demise. But when she gets to the funeral, Mary can't control her giggles until she's overtaken by laughter. Does this seem to be an inappropriate time and place for Mary to be laughing? Maybe. We're uncomfortable when we are around emotion of any kind.

Yet when someone else determines that it's "OK," we will allow ourselves to bring in that emotion. It's "OK" to cry at a wedding. It's "OK" to scream at a basketball game. It's "OK" to laugh hysterically at slapstick comedy. But cross that line and bring one of those emotions into an unfamiliar setting, and it's not "OK."

Who said? Who said you can't bring all of yourself to a situation? Is it because it makes other people uncomfortable and those other people are the ones who make the rules?

I'd rather have a living, breathing, emoting human being in my workplace or as a friend than a straight-faced automaton.

When you ask someone to bring their passion for their job – you want them to do the best job they can and bring all of their passion with them – you have to be prepared for the whole person to join them.

Perhaps the challenge we have is with the word "passion." What is the connotation of that word? The true meaning is "a strong feeling or emotion; boundless enthusiasm." Christians use the word to mean the suffering of Jesus, yet it appears only once in the Bible in this context in Acts 1:3. It also means "any violent or intense emotion that prevents reflection" as in the term "crime of passion."

So given that definition, maybe we don't really want passion at all. If we think passion is a "soft" word that intimidates us, what we think is what will occur for us. What we think is what we become. The diagram below shows this as a circular relationship. What we think is what we create; what we create is what we become; what we become is what we express; what we express is what we experience; what we experience is what we are; and what we are is what we think.

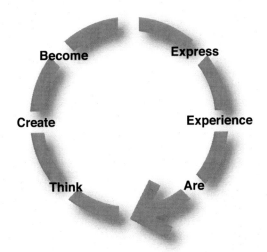

Have you ever thought about that saying about getting up on the wrong side of the bed? Have you ever had a day that started out badly and just got worse? You just know your hair will look terrible, you'll stub your toe on the bed and the coffee will spill as you're pouring it.

On the other hand, have you ever had a day where everything just clicked? You were on a roll and the world was your oyster – and everything just fell into place perfectly.

Well, one thing those days have in common, despite the differences in the outward appearance, is you. You really can choose the attitude you're going to take with you through the rest of the day. When you discover that you're doing things effortlessly and enjoying them to the fullest, you may just have connected with your passion. And if you can find the good things even when the days don't appear to be going so well, then maybe your passion has something to do with just that: finding the silver lining in every cloud.

Thomas Jefferson, one of our country's founding fathers, believed that each of us is entitled to certain inalienable rights, including Life, Liberty, and the pursuit of Happiness.

Ah, how quickly we forget about our inalienable right to be happy! There seem to be so many times and circumstances where we are unconsciously giving up our right to be happy to feed the need to be right. How ironic.

I can believe that no one will want to listen to my idea, or ask me on a date, or hire me for a job, and then do everything in my power to prove it so I can be right. Never mind that stepping outside the familiar zone (I believe it's no longer comfortable there) will almost always yield better outcomes than those I can get while in the midst of those familiar ruts.

I propose that it's the pursuit of happiness that leaves us unhappy. If we could just be happy, we wouldn't have to be in pursuit of something to make us happy. Just choose. Don't worry. Be happy. Choose it - NOW, not someday!

The Universal Laws, especially the Law of Attraction, have gained popularity in recent years, even though they are not new concepts. The global phenomenon *The Secret* has opened up a new conversation in everyday life about this force which attracts to us those people, things, situations which we think about most often. There is actually science behind this law and several new – and not-so-new – books have grabbed my attention and added to my knowledge on this topic.

The first book I remember coming into my space regarding this law was *As A Man Thinketh* by James Allen, which was given to me by a client. This book was first published in 1902, so it's certainly not new to the world, even though it was new to me. Other books in this genre and of a similar timeframe include Wallace Wattles' *The Science of Getting Rich* (1910) and *Your Invisible Power* by Genevieve Behrand (1921).

All of these books, and many others of that timeframe right up to the present moment, focus on our ability to attract what we want by being aware of and then choosing how we think. Of course anything that challenges traditional ways of doing or thinking will be met with an equal and opposing force, and positive thinking and visualization is no exception. However, when we consider that the Law of Attraction really works whether we believe it or not, we come to see that we really do get what we think about most, whether that's in opposition of something or in favor of something.

When people say they have a passion for anything, it's probably something that makes them feel good deep down to their core, and that usually makes people happy. But happiness isn't the goal – it's the outcome of connecting with that passion. Many people identify that passion when they begin to deal in heightened awareness – when they begin to notice things differently. So becoming more aware of the things around us seems to lead us to new choices in our thought process.

What you spend your time thinking about really does have a way of making itself into your everyday existence. So if you're still searching for your passion, maybe part of the secret is to find passion in the everyday things. When you get familiar with what passion feels like in your body, you'll be more apt to recognize the flashes when they show up.

Think about what it is you want. Then move it to what you intend. This will start the circle for you in your own life. As you become what you think, you can go beyond the meaning of the word to the context you create. You'll find that this can become your own version of passion.

REALITY CHECKLIST

(complete and repeat as needed)

What's my definition of passion? What am I passionate about? _____

_____

_____

_____

_____

How do I express my passion? _____

_____

_____

_____

How is it working? _____

_____

_____

_____

What might I do differently? _____

_____

_____

_____

The CREATIVITY and COURAGE CONUNDRUM

"Keep away from people who try to belittle your ambitions. Small people always do that, but the really great make you feel that you, too, can become great."

~ Mark Twain

G etting beyond what others think is a huge victory. And even the belief that those "others" might be out there judging new endeavors is often enough to keep us in status quo behavior even when we know it's not the best solution.

This seems to be especially true when it comes to creativity. I didn't realize how difficult it really is to define creativity until I started to think more about it. My own definition would be something like: the ability to create; inventing something new; or coming up with fresh ideas. I used to think that people were either born creative or they weren't, and that creative people were those people who could draw, or paint, or act, or write.

I believe now that the level of my own creativity was in direct proportion to my level of courage. I spent so much of my youth as a perfectionist that I had very little space to be creative. Being creative to me now means being willing to step outside the traditional into the unknown. It means being willing to make a mistake - to take a risk - to get beyond worrying about what others think and following what I think.

As I've started listening to my life speak, I find that my true self is, as some have called me, a boat rocker - a limb sitter - a trailblazer. I've found it to be much easier to follow my heart than to feel pressured to justify my existence in a work environment that doesn't know what to do with me.

I believe that everyone has the ability to be creative. But in order for people to connect with their innate creativity, there has to be some semblance of courage present as well. Many of us don't have enough experience out on the limb or outside the status quo to even know how to support someone who's venturing out there. It might seem to be lonely out on the limb. But it's much less lonely when you find others in the same place than it is to be struggling alone amid other closet creatives, none of whom is yet ready or willing to venture into the unknown.

Living creatively = living courageously.

But being creative does not have to mean artistic. That may be where some of us get hung up. The root of the word "creativity" is "creation." Starting from nothing. Creating something new.

So what does it really mean to be creative? One of my favorite books is *Orbiting the Giant Hairball* by Gordon MacKenzie, a sketch artist at Hallmark for 30 years. Gordon says that in order to survive, a society has traditionally needed a vision of what it means to be normal.

He says that creativity, which he uses interchangeably with "genius," is not so much about being normal as being original. Gordon says our creative genius fires our compulsion to evolve. It inspires us to challenge norms. Creative genius is about flying to new heights on untested wings. It is all about the danger of crashing.

But our society does not know how to handle creative genius. From the time we are old enough to talk, we learn the word NO – we learn that we must do everything we can do to be "normal."

Those who manage to get beyond those words are ostracized, teased, and outcast. They're called "eccentric" and "weird" and "free-spirited" and "odd."

In my youth I did anything and everything I could do to be accepted – even if it meant reining in my own creativity. Although it wasn't always comfortable to suppress my ideas, it was more uncomfortable to have everyone else think I was different from them.

I think the lack of comfort gave way to the familiarity that took over in my life. I remember several times throughout my career when I found myself waiting desperately for someone in authority to "discover" my creativity and give me permission to be who I knew I was deep down inside. But of course, that never happened. It's only again in my 20/20 hindsight that I realize that creativity is threatening to authority. We've been raised to believe – whether consciously or not – that knowledge is power, and giving up knowledge, especially to people who might think more creatively than fear-based worldviews allow, will be giving up power.

In my work now with individuals and teams within organizations, one of the first questions I ask has to do with their reaction to and identification with fear. What I find is that often it's very difficult for them to identify exactly what this fear is – or even what it is based on.

Are we afraid of speaking up and saying what's on our minds? Fear is a strong emotion, and strong emotion – energy in motion – is creative. The way to live without fear is to know that every outcome in life is perfect just the way it is.

In spite of our best efforts, our entire universe is creative. It is constantly creating something. When you cut your finger, it automatically heals. The seasons come and go, the sun comes up in the east and sets in the west, even if we don't want it to. It happens in spite of us. Yet we keep trying to interfere in the creative process – the process of creating – by asserting our knowledge and thus, our perceived power.

When I was a little kid, I used to love to go to the park and swing on the huge metal swing set. The higher I could swing, the better. I'd pump my legs back underneath the seat as hard as I could so I could get to the top of the swing and hit that little moment of being airborn, and swing back and do it again.

So, how high would I have been able to swing if I had decided that the backswing was bad? How much momentum would I have been able to generate if every time I pushed forward, I dug my heels into the ground at the midpoint to stop from swinging backward? I would be using all my energy to push forward, and then even more energy to avoid going backward and would never get that rush of flying free.

We can all relate to this analogy from our childhood, but how many of us realize that this is what we are doing with our own creativity? Creation is the forward motion – the upswing. Destruction is the backswing of that pendulum. Somewhere along the line we decided that only the forward or creative swing is valuable. We resist the other half of the cycle – either because of our conditioning or our fear – and we break our momentum and waste our creative energy. We forget that when we create music, we destroy silence. When we create art, we destroy blank canvas. When we create knowledge, we destroy ignorance.

I watched an episode of TLC's *Clean Sweep* about a woman who was very attached to an old table which was taking up valuable space in her house. But the table, an antique left to her from her grandparents, represented the mess her life had become because of her inability to get rid of old things. She needed to physically destroy the table in order to create a new beginning – not only in her house, but in her life.

So often we spend our time stuffing information, knowledge, advice in to our heads that we don't allow ourselves time to let it out; to create something from scratch; to start over.

That may be why education seems to have stopped being a creative experience for our children. We stuff information into their heads, and don't allow them to bring any of it out. In the book *The Prime of Miss Jean Brodie*, Miss Brodie says that:

> *The word 'education' comes from the root e from ex, out, and duco, I lead. It means a leading out. To me education is a leading out of what is already there in the pupil's soul. To Miss Mackay it is a putting in of something that is not there, and that is not what I call education. I call it intrusion.*

Some of my favorite movies have been about educators who promote creative learning for their students. Consider *Dead Poet's Society* where Mr. Keating, the teacher played by Robin Williams, says to the students: "I stand upon my desk to remind myself that we must constantly look at things in a different way." That takes courage and yields creativity.

Or *Mona Lisa Smile* where Katherine Watson, the teacher played by Julia Roberts, says to her students: "I thought that I was headed to a place that would turn out tomorrow's leaders, not their wives." That takes courage and yields creativity.

Or *Mr. Holland's Opus* where Mr. Holland, the music teacher played by Richard Dreyfus, says: "Playing music is supposed to be fun. It's about heart, it's about feelings, moving people, and something beautiful, and it's not about notes on a page. I can teach you notes on a page, I can't teach you that other stuff." That, too, takes courage and yields creativity.

Think about the areas of your creativity that you avoid. Do you hate to make a mess? Are you constantly straightening and organizing when you need to crumple the paper? Do you waste time trying to find supplies in the cupboard you never make time to organize? Are you afraid of making a mistake? Are you so focused on getting the beginning just right that you never move on to the middle and the end of the project? Do you pull out so many imperfect stitches that you never finish the quilt? Or do you throw things together quickly and promise yourself that someday you'll do it right? What are you afraid of ruining, wrecking, destroying? Where do you stop your momentum? Where do you drag your feet and dig your heels in?

Sure, it's going to take some courage to get beyond your own status quo. But isn't the potential payoff worth the risk?

Although the sayings on the T-shirts from No Fear Gear have gotten much edgier in recent years, I've got two of them in my closet left over from my playing days. One says "You can't steal second base with one foot on first." And the other one says "I don't practice to come in second." Even though those shirts are several years old, and have made it through countless basketball, volleyball and softball games, the messages are great reminders to me about taking some chances in order to get new results.

I have a friend who used to run a mosaic shop called Big Break Amusing Mosaics. The idea behind Big Break is that people can show up there to break ceramic tiles, old plates, cups, saucers and such, and then create works of art from the destruction.

I invited some friends to join me at Big Break to create some art and the first thing I noticed when we all got there was that there was an almost tangible air of anxiety among my friends, along with the feeling that they were under pressure to be creative among all the pretty colors and books of inspirational ideas from others who are undoubtedly more inherently creative than any of us thought we were.

But it didn't take long for the breaking, bashing, nipping, clipping, cementing, and yes, creating to happen (of course the wine didn't hurt!). Two hours into our projects all of us were amazed at the beauty we had created.

This is a great analogy for most of our lives at work and at home. When it comes right down to it, we really are capable of much more than we can initially see in the midst of the problems, chaos, upset and even destruction of our lives. How often do we give ourselves permission to get in there and get dirty, much less to celebrate the inevitable victories we either witness or create?

If you're afraid to be creative because you're conditioned to believe that only positive motion is creative, consider Big Break. You have to destroy to create. You have to be willing to get beyond your fears to connect with what you really can do. The beauty that can come out of the seeming destruction will give you a new experience – and new knowledge about your capacity.

REALITY CHECKLIST

(complete and repeat as needed)

How do I define creativity? What's creative in my life? _____

_____

_____

_____

_____

What am I doing to identify with my creativity? _____

_____

_____

_____

_____

How is it working? _____

_____

_____

_____

_____

What might I do differently? _____

_____

_____

_____

_____

The PERILS OF PRESENCE

**"Seventy percent of success in life
is showing up."**

~ Woody Allen

R emember the old Ralph Edwards show *This Is Your Life*, a semi-documentary-style program where the lives of show-business personalities, who appear as guests, are relived through the testimonies of friends and family? Maybe I'm showing my age, but I vaguely remember the host reading from a big book the highlights of some celebrity's life and then voices coming from backstage telling stories about the person, and then re-uniting for a wonderful homecoming celebration.

How often do people get the chance to 1) have their life's accomplishments recognized and celebrated in this way and 2) to be part of celebrating someone else's life's accomplishments? Usually this is what funerals or wakes are for, right? Isn't it strange that our customs are set up to celebrate and acknowledge us when we're not even around to appreciate it?

Just think about the amazing clarity those four words have the potential to provide. THIS - IS - YOUR - LIFE. No more. No less. This is it. You can even get a slightly different context for yourself if you shift the emphasis. THIS - is - your - life. This - IS - your - life. This - is - YOUR - life. And this - is - your - LIFE. Try each of those on. Do you see what I mean?

I'm reminded of how important it is for us to remember that for ourselves. It really affects the way we live (or exist), the way we work (or survive), the way we play (or sulk), and the way we respond (or blame).

In his book *Work 2.0: Rewriting the Contract*, Bill Jensen writes about how "more than ever before, we're rediscovering that people do matter! The human-side of the equation still drives productivity, efficiency, and business results" (from the book jacket).

Work 2.0 is about a new work contract that employees can write as they look for work that lights them up and makes them come alive.

It may sound a bit radical to state our needs as employees. Bill warns in the welcome of the book: "This is a book for doers. Builders. Leaders who are willing to get their fingernails dirty in the details....It is a book for people who are willing to put their values and passions, as well as their accountabilities, on the line."

But, after all, This Is Your Life.

Celebrate who you are - and celebrate with others. Life is too short - and too long - to spend your days, hours, minutes, doing things that don't resonate with you – that don't light you up. If we aren't able to articulate our own wants and needs, how can we expect others to do that for us? They can't read our minds - especially if we haven't got a clear message to put out there for them.

Some of the challenges we face in our daily lives come from inside our own heads. Research has shown that we have 60,000 random thoughts going through our heads on any given day and a great majority of those thoughts are the same ones we had the day before. We end up getting stuck in our own rut and the voices in our heads want to keep us stuck. If we're listening to those thoughts, we're not present to the reality that is occurring around us.

The effect of those voices in our heads also shows up in the quality of our listening. Have you ever been in a conversation with someone and realized that you missed a lot of what the he was saying because you were listening to your own thoughts?

Here are some questions to ask yourself to determine how present you are in conversation. Just noticing your listening tendencies might give you some ideas on what you might do differently.

- Do I tend not to listen to people with whom I disagree?
- Do I find it difficult to fully participate in conversations where the subject is not of interest to me?
- When I feel I know the message the talker is trying to get across, do I stop listening?
- Do I ask people to clarify things I don't understand?
- Do I usually form a rebuttal in my head while the other person is talking?
- If I'm not listening, do I tell the person or ask him to repeat what I missed?
- Do I make eye contact with the person who is talking?

What are you doing to enjoy and fully live in the present? If, as Woody Allen says, 70% is in the showing up, how are you showing up? Grudgingly? Resentfully? Tentatively? Or are you living today as if today is all you've got? It really is, you know. And it's truly a gift. That's why they call it the PRESENT!

REALITY CHECKLIST

(complete and repeat as needed)

Which areas of my life could benefit from my being more present? _____

_____

_____

_____

_____

What am I doing to increase my presence? _____

_____

_____

_____

How is it working? _____

_____

_____

_____

_____

What might I do differently? _____

_____

_____

_____

_____

The GLORY of GRATITUDE

"As we express our gratitude, we must never forget that the highest appreciation is not to utter words, but to live by them."

~ John F. Kennedy

S top right now and think – just for a minute – about what you are grateful for. Right now. In this moment. Take a deep breath. Were you able to take in that sweet air easily and comfortably? Be grateful for that.

Take a look around you, wherever you are right now. What colors do you notice? Even when the sky appears to be gray, the reality is that it is always blue way beyond the clouds. Be grateful for that.

Think of all the people in your life. Even that less-than-positive server at the busy restaurant or your crabby Uncle Charley. They're all there to teach you some sort of lesson – a lesson in forgiveness, in love, in compassion, in gratitude. Be grateful for them.

I attended a learning circle event in which the participants all shared observations about their lives. One of the most profound insights I received at that event was from a 14-year-old who shared something he had been noticing. He said that he was thinking about something the teacher who was conducting the learning circle had once told him. She had said that if he didn't have something, he really didn't need it.

This 14-year-old had been thinking about that as it relates to his father, who is not present in his life. He said if he had known his father, he wouldn't have the relationship he has with his mother and her parents (his grandparents) who have been studying with this teacher for several years. He realized that he also wouldn't have learned the things he's learning from this teacher and probably wouldn't have the awareness he has in his own happiness.

That from a 14-year-old.

During that same learning circle, the teacher asked us if we recognized the distinction between gratitude and thankfulness. That question in itself invited a lot of very interesting dialogue, and what we determined is that thanks is something you offer for things or situations you have already received. Gratitude, on the other hand, is a way of being. Instead of reacting to something that has already happened, gratitude is being aware of and appreciating things and situations even though the outcome may not be what you think you want, or may not be happening in your timeframe.

If we are committed to seeing the world through the eyes of gratitude, we will see everything differently. We really will notice that there are so many more things, situations, people and even trials and tribulations that we can see are for our higher good in the big picture.

The teacher gave us a challenge to help us actually experience the distinction between gratitude and thankfulness. She encouraged us to take on a 30-day project in which we create a list of 30 things to be grateful for – anything from a material object to a dear family member to a life experience. Once the list is created, the idea is to journal about one of those topics a day for the next 30 days.

Take a tuna sandwich, to use her example. The challenge encourages us to take the time, whenever we find ourselves with a break in our thought process, to be aware of and grateful for absolutely every detail of that tuna sandwich – from the bread that surrounds the tuna to the boat used by the fishermen to catch the fish.

Daniel Pink gives a couple more ideas for developing an attitude of gratitude in his book *A Whole New Mind*. There he tells about the "gratitude one-a-day" and the "birthday gratitude list." The birthday gratitude list is simply a list you make, each year on your birthday, of things you're grateful for. Because you make this list each year on your birthday, the number of items on the list needs to equal the number of years you're turning that day, so each year the list gets one item longer. Dan suggests keeping the lists and reviewing them each birthday. Sounds like a great idea to me.

The gratitude one-a-day has us get into the habit whenever we're doing something we do every day - making the bed, having the morning coffee, stretching before getting up – of thinking of one thing for which we're grateful. Just like those rituals, the idea of gratitude becomes a habit – and one that we don't want to break.

When we become more comfortable and familiar with the attitude of gratitude, we see that eventually our entire outlook becomes one of hopeful and happy anticipation instead of doom and gloom.

Even situations which we think are negative can be seen through an entirely different filter.

For some reason (and I'm sure there is one) the term "Pollyanna" has been dancing around in my head recently. My initial reaction to that term brings up a person who is idealistic and outside the realm of reality, as in "quit being such a Pollyanna."

My only personal context of Pollyanna is from the 1960 Disney film starring Hayley Mills, but the movie was based on the 1913 novel by Eleanor Porter. To make a long story short, Pollyanna is a young girl who always has a positive outlook on life, even though she's had a lot of adversities to overcome. She is sent to live with her Aunt Polly, a wealthy and prominent woman who is very much a glass-half-empty kind of person. Pollyanna brings with her a game she learned from her father called the "Glad Game" in which she always finds the good in any situation. In fact, her father gave her a brooch with this inscription on it:

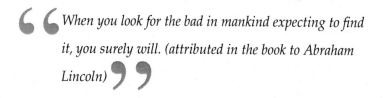

When you look for the bad in mankind expecting to find it, you surely will. (attributed in the book to Abraham Lincoln)

So when Pollyanna is sent to live with her aunt in the town of Beldingsville, which, since her aunt pretty much runs the town, has taken on her dour attitude, we see how one young, positive girl can actually change the entire town. Despite the fact that her aunt puts her in a stuffy attic room without carpets or pictures, Pollyanna is glad for the wonderful view out the window from her high perch.

When her aunt punishes her for being late to dinner by making her eat bread and milk in the kitchen with Nancy, the servant, Pollyanna thanks her aunt because she likes bread and milk and she likes Nancy.

Doesn't this remind you of another young girl who saw the good in the world despite her own situation? I'm thinking of Anne Frank, whose story is certainly one you've heard, but which wouldn't hurt to revisit.

So what's wrong with being a Pollyanna? Seeing the good in every situation by playing the "Glad Game" can't be a bad way to see the world, can it? The cynics of the world may call you naive and they may fight to be right about their cynical attitude. As Richard Bach said in *Illusions*: "Argue for your limitations and sure enough, they're yours."

Viktor Frankl's story of surviving a German concentration camp during World War II, which he tells in his book *Man's Search for Meaning*, and Immaculee Ilibagiza's story of surviving the Rwandan holocaust which she tells in her book *Left to Tell*, are two other examples of the power of gratitude in even life and death situations.

This chapter on gratitude really does sum up most of the thoughts throughout this entire book. You can see how being personally accountable for results in your life and making up your mind to change your mind really can give you a new perspective. Using gratitude as the lens through which you see the world will give you tangible evidence that all problems are in the past and all solutions are right now. Even the future is beyond our ability to control, except by creating the attitude with which we will head into that future.

By noticing everything that comes into your awareness and being grateful even for the smallest aspect you can come up with at the time, you will begin to develop your own mental muscles of thanks, praise, gratitude and perception.

Pick a strategy. It might be the "Glad Game" or it might be creating your own gratitude journal and taking on the gratitude challenge. Maybe it's the gratitude one-a-day or the birthday gratitude list. Or simply select someone for whom you are truly grateful in your life and write that person a letter. I am grateful now that when my favorite college professor retired, I wrote him a heartfelt letter in gratitude – and yes, in thanks – for the worlds he had opened up for me. A few years later I spoke at his memorial service about the attitude of gratitude I had developed because of his presence in my life. I am grateful even today that I wrote that letter and he received it before he died. Even though he is no longer physically alive, I believe I am a better person because of his inspiration. That feeling I'm experiencing even as I write this is gratitude.

Because gratitude is more a way of being than an act of doing, it sometimes can be difficult to notice. We tend to get so caught up in our own busyness that we take for granted some of the things for which we can be most grateful. If we don't have many material goods, we may feel victimized and not be in a state of gratitude. On the other hand, if we have never known a life without many material goods, we may not appreciate where we are. It's the old story of standing on third base in your life and thinking you hit a triple, when in fact it has taken the effort, the love, and the support many people to get you where you are.

My good friends Darcy Simonson and Sheila Sornsin understand the concept of gratitude. In fact, they formed their own company called *The Grateful Goddess* (www.thegratefulgoddess.com) to celebrate the gratitude we can all experience if we're just aware.

Through whimsical art, jewelry and in-person gatherings, Darcy and Sheila celebrate this attitude of gratitude, and encourage others to shift their focus to do the same in their own lives.

Stop. Be present. Think. Be accountable, authentic, and just notice. Where are you? Who are you? What do you really, really want? Start today by being grateful for where and who you are. As Lao-Tzu told us more than 2,500 years ago: "The journey of a thousand miles begins with a single step." Take that step in gratitude and you'll be amazed at the sights you'll see.

REALITY CHECKLIST

(complete and repeat as needed)

For what or whom am I most grateful in my life? _____

_____

_____

_____

_____

What am I doing to express my gratitude – both internally and externally?

_____

_____

_____

_____

How is it working? _____

_____

_____

_____

_____

What might I do differently? _____

_____

_____

_____

_____

Afterword

E ach chapter of this book addresses some aspect of your life by relaying wisdom you've heard before. Whether it's reducing fear, building courage, acknowledging accountability, or enhancing communication, you probably already know a lot of the stuff you've read about here.

The question you can ask yourself is, if I *know* it, why am I not *doing* something with it?

Do you know the size of your container? Are you in touch with yourself enough to be able to take inventory and find out? And be honest about it? Are you able to quit comparing yourself to others and do and be what you know you were meant to do and be?

Why is it so difficult to do what we know? Do we need to stand on the brink of our own knowing long enough to come into our own acceptance? Do we need to try new ideas out long enough to be able to overcome the voice of reason and experience that either lives inside of us or outside of us through our bosses, teachers, parents, co-workers, relatives? As we come into our own voice, and our own knowing, we may be surprised to find that others are there just waiting for us to show the way. And still others will be there with hands outstretched to help guide us. We're not in this alone.

Don't wait for someday. Don't wait for a tragedy to force you to do what you know. What will it take? It doesn't have to be overwhelming. "Life is hard by the yard, but by the inch, life's a cinch." Baby steps taken in a forward direction are still steps. However, according to the website *Notes from the Universe* (www.tut.com), "The difference between taking baby steps and acting small is that one prepares you for success, the other for a fall."

So here are some ideas to get you thinking beyond where you are today:

- *Instead of telling someone an answer, ask a question. Be genuinely interested in the answer you get.*

- Be still and be quiet. Get in touch with the voices in your head. Identify which is the "victim" voice, which is the "villain" voice, and which is the voice of your own Higher Self.

- *Get beyond the practical and explore the possible.*

- Notice what you notice.

- *Enhance your awareness and mindfulness.*

- Trust your own knowing.

- *Encourage dialogue for the purpose of learning from others,
  but don't rely on others for your own answers.*

- Be aware of your intentions. The only person you can change
  is you, but you can influence and affect many others
  – sometimes without even realizing it.

- *Get in the game—and maximize your capacity with each endeavor!*

You have the opportunity to expand your capacities in many areas – your capacity to understand, to create, to communicate, to earn, to feel, to believe, to act. But there is just one way to live fully, and that is to live at 100% capacity in whichever area that is today, not sometime in the future.

Concentrate on the percentage instead of the potential. Live your 100% regardless of how it measures up to someone else's 100%. If you're living at full capacity in the moment, you're living at maximum capacity.

One of the great ironies of living on purpose, in the moment, is that while you're concentrating on the task at hand – living without expectation or attachment – the universe is conspiring to bring you expanded capacity in all areas of your life. The real secret: **YOU REALLY DON'T EVEN HAVE TO DO ANYTHING!** If you're fully present your capacity automatically grows.

The beauty of the journey of life is that it is a process, not an event. If you can look at this journey as a trip, say, from New York to San Francisco, you know that there are many ways to get there. If it is imperative that you get to San Francisco quickly, you'll travel the most direct route. If you decide that you'd like to take some time to see the sights and experience all there is to experience along the way, you might start from New York, but travel to Florida, down the coast to Texas, across the border to Mexico, head back up toward North Dakota, maybe venture into Canada, and eventually work your way down the west coast to your final destination.

What if the destination is guaranteed, regardless of the route you choose to get there? How might that alter the scenery? How might you see that you really do have a say in how you get to San Francisco despite the roadblocks and potholes and heavy traffic and long, lonely stretches of back roads?

Choose, today, to get out the roadmap and create a more mindful route by living your capacity with every task and every project and every encounter you experience. Start with a small container and fill it up to 100% and recreate that feeling as you increase your capacity.

Oh, and make sure to enjoy the ride!

Ideas for Living at Full Capacity

The time of life is short!/To spend that shortness basely were too long.
– Shakespeare

When you were born, you cried and the world rejoiced
Live your life in such a manner that when you die
the world cries and you rejoice.
– Indian proverb

Life is either a daring adventure or nothing. To keep our faces toward change
and behave like free spirits in the presence of fate is strength undefeatable.
– Helen Keller

Always dream and shoot higher than you know you can do.
Don't bother just to be better than your contemporaries or
predecessors. Try to be better than yourself.
– William Faulkner

The secret of getting ahead is getting started. The secret of getting started
is breaking your complex overwhelming tasks into small manageable tasks,
and then starting on the first one.
– Mark Twain

If I am not for myself, who will be for me?
If I am only for myself, what am I?
If not now—when?
– Hillel the Elder

All big things in this world are done by people who are naïve and have an idea that is obviously impossible.
– Dr. Frank Richards

A year from now you may wish you had started today.
– Karen Lamb

You cannot discover oceans unless you have the courage to reach the shore.
You can't steal second base with one foot on first.
–Unknown

I shall be telling this with a sigh
Somewhere ages and ages hence;
Two roads diverged in a wood, and I—
I took the one less traveled by,
And that has made all the difference.
– Robert Frost

It's never too late to be what you might have been.
– George Eliot

If you do follow your bliss, you put yourself on a kind of track that has been there all the while, waiting for you, and the life you ought to be living is the one you are living.
– Joseph Campbell

When I stand before God at the end of my life, I would hope that
I would not have a single bit of talent left, and could say,
"I used everything you gave me."
— Erma Bombeck

Be who you are and say what you feel, because those who mind don't
matter and those who matter don't mind.
— Dr. Seuss

There is a vitality, a life force, an energy, a quickening, that is translated
through you into action, and because there is only one of you in all time,
this expression is unique. And if you block it, it will never exist through any
other medium and will be lost.
— Martha Graham

Do not spoil what you have by desiring what
you have not; but remember that what you now have
was once among the things only hoped for.
— Epicurus

Books Mentioned in The 100% Factor

Adams, Marilee G. *Change Your Questions, Change Your Life: 7 Powerful Tools for Life and Work*. Berrett-Koehler Publishers, 2004.

Bane, Rosanne. *Dancing in the Dragon's Den: Rekindling the Creative Fire in Your Shadow*. Weiser Books. 1999.

Blanke, Gail. *Between Trapezes: Flying Into a New Life With The Greatest of Ease*. Rodale Books, 2004.

Buckingham, Marcus and Coffman, Curt. *First Break All the Rules: What the World's Greatest Managers Do Differently*. Simon & Shuster, 1999.

Cooper, Robert K. *The Other 90%: How to Unlock Your Vast Untapped Potential for Leadership and Life*. Crown Business, 2001.

Farber, Steve. *The Radical Leap: A Personal Lesson in Extreme Leadership*. Kaplan Business, 2004.

Frankl, Viktor E. *Man's Search for Meaning*. Beacon Press, 2006.

Godin, Seth. *Survival is Not Enough: Zooming, Evolution, and the Future of Your Company*. Free Press, First Edition, 2002.

Ilibagiza, Immaculee. *Left to Tell: Discovering God Amidst the Rwandan Holocaust*. Hay House, 2007.

Jensen, Bill. *Work 2.0: Rewriting the Contract*. Perseus Books, 2002.

MacKenzie, Gordon. *Orbiting the Giant Hairball: A Corporate Fool's Guide to Surviving With Grace*. Viking, 1998.

Pink, Daniel H. *A Whole New Mind: Why Right-Brainers Will Rule the Future*. Penguin Books, 2006.

Ruiz, don Miguel. *The Four Agreements*. Amber-Allen Publishing, 1997.

Secretan, Lance. *Inspire! What Great Leaders Do*. Wiley, 2004.

Spark, Muriel. *The Prime of Miss Jean Brodie*. 1st Perennial Classics edition, 1999.

Walsch, Neale Donald. *Communion With God: An Uncommon Dialogue*. Putnam, 2000.

Whyte, David. *The Heart Aroused: Poetry and the Preservation of the Soul in Corporate America*. Currency, 1996.

Williamson, Marianne. *A Return to Love*. Harper, 1996.

Acknowledgements

I've been privileged to work with some wonderful clients since the first printing of this book in 2006, and their interest in this book has made this third printing possible (and necessary). Thank you to each and every one. In addition to everyone who helped make the first edition possible, I'd like to add my continued thanks to my posse – Carolyn, Michael, Gina & Cary - for keeping the Spirit alive. To the Miracles Mafia – thank you for demonstrating the power of trust and love – and miracles! To my business partner Merrill – thanks for continuing to live your own genius for the benefit of all our current and future clients. To all my master mind participants – you are amazing. Thank you for trusting in the vision of *Think And Grow Rich!* and taking it beyond study to application. I'd name you all here but I trust the list will continue to grow. And finally, thank you to my family – Mom, Patti, Larry, Logan & Codi - who allowed me to learn a lot of great lessons over the years, and who continue to support me in my learning and growth.

As Rosanne Bane pointed out in her book, *Dancing in the Dragon's Den*, the main reason anyone would read the acknowledgements is to see whether they were mentioned. So I'd like to invite you to fill in the blank with your own name, because without you, the reader, there would be no reason for writing the book. So thank you, _____, for your interest in reading *The 100% Factor* – and even more for doing whatever you can to make your own small talk bigger. Collectively we can make a difference in the world by what we think, create, become, express, and experience!

A Final Note

If you'd like more information about living your capacity, check out my blog at http://youalreadyknowthisstuff.blogspot.com. There you will find a plethora of ideas and recommended reading as well as a list of other bloggers who share many of my ideas and provide a fabulous sounding board (well, typing board) for meaningful dialogue.

If you'd like to continue the dialogue, grab this book and head over to your favorite coffee shop with a good friend and ask each other what you want and what you're doing to get it. Create your own team to cheer each other on as you accomplish the goals you set for yourself. Get a little notebook for your purse or pocket and record what you're seeing and share your victories.

You'll be amazed at how different the scenery is when you're looking from a new perspective!

About The Author

Jodee Bock is owner of Bock's Office Transformational Consulting in Fargo, North Dakota. Bock's Office supports individuals and teams in succeeding in whatever they are committed to accomplishing. They provide customized training, facilitation, and keynote speaking on topics like leadership, personal accountability, effectiveness, creativity and innovation, authenticity, and change.

Jodee spent more than 15 years in many facets of Corporate America, including careers as a newspaper editor, sports information director, corporate communicator, PR manager, corporate trainer, and management consultant. She is a college basketball All-American, sings in an award-winning barbershop chorus, and is passionate about seeing people connect with their purpose and destiny.

She is co-author of the book *Don't Miss Your Boat: Living Your Life With Purpose in the Real World* (Aloha Publishing 2004). This is her first solo book.

For more information about Jodee's speaking, training and facilitation, contact her at jodee@bocksoffice.com or visit her website at www.bocksoffice.com.